Foreword by Teddy Ngbanda

GETTING OUT OF BAD DEBT

Hubert Ayanou

Copyright © 2025 Hubert Ayanou

No part of this book may be reproduced, distributed, or transmitted in any form or by any means, including photocopying, recording, or other electronic or mechanical methods, without the prior written permission of the publisher and the author, except in the case of brief quotations used in reviews or certain other non-commercial uses permitted by copyright law.

Publisher: Upway Books
Authors: Hubert Ayanou
Title: GETTING OUT OF BAD DEBT
ISBN: 978-1-917916-36-3
Cover Designed on Canva: www.canva.com

This book is a work of non-fiction. The information it contains is based on the author's research, experience, and knowledge at the time of publication. The publisher and authors have made every effort to ensure the accuracy and reliability of the information provided, but assume no responsibility for any errors, omissions, or differing interpretations of the subject matter. This publication is not intended to replace professional advice or consultation. Readers are encouraged to seek professional guidance where appropriate.

contact@upwaybooks.com
www.upwaybooks.com

Original edition published in French under the original title:
Comment Sortir Des Mauvaises Dettes

TABLE OF CONTENTS

DEDICATION 5

FOREWORD 7

INTRODUCTION 9

Chapter 1: MAKING A DIFFERENCE BETWEEN BAD AND GOOD DEBT 11

Chapter 2: SOURCES OF BAD DEBT.. 27

Chapter 3: ARE YOU IN DEBT? NINE QUESTIONS TO FIND OUT 33

Chapter 4: THE CONSEQUENCES OF BAD DEBT 39

Chapter 5: SUPERFICIAL FIXES TO DEBT....................................... 45

Chapter 6: DOWN WITH PROCRASTINATION! 51

Chapter 7: PRACTICAL ADVICE TO GET OUT OF BAD DEBT 59

Chapter 8: CREATE WEALTH WITH THIS INGRAINED HABIT!................. 91

Chapter 9: BREAK THE HEREDITARY CIRCLE OF PRECARIOUSNESS AND RESTORE THE FINANCIAL FLOW OF JUSTICE................................. 99

DEDICATION

To all who wish to free themselves from bad debt
to achieve financial freedom and independence;

To all who aspire to be true creators of wealth in their generation;

May you find in this book the practical keys to break
out of ignorance and find balance in your finances.

FOREWORD

Personal finance or money is generally one of the most important and delicate topics to tackle. Daily, many people are faced with situations linked to debt and poor management of their financial resources. The good news is that it is possible to overcome debt and reclaim financial freedom. I highly recommend '*Getting out of Bad Debt*'.

The Bible, which is full of words of inspiration on all subjects, says this:

"Shall not all these take up their taunt against him, with scoffing and riddles for him, and say, 'Woe to him who heaps up what is not his own – for how long? – and loads himself with pledges!'" (**Habakkuk 2:6**)

As a servant of God, I firmly believe that we must be sound financial stewards and wise in the management of the resources that God places at our disposal. Bad debt is a burden on the head of anyone who incurs them and therefore a subject of constant mockery and worry. Anyone who wants to fully and effectively fulfil his or her destiny must educate him- or herself financially and to apply the biblical principles of financial management.

This book is a goldmine of advice combined with proven strategies to help you understand the nature of debt and develop a concrete plan to free yourself from it. It takes a personal decision and discipline to change your status by applying the contents of this book.

In what follows, Hubert Ayanou takes us through an inventory of our current finances. His aim is to guide us in making wise and enlightened decisions to achieve effective prosperity. He shares methods for drawing up budgets and practical keys to getting rid of bad debt and achieving financial freedom.

I am convinced that God is raising up economically equipped people in this generation to free His children from the yoke of debt. As you read this book, keep an open mind and be honest with yourself by doing the practical exercises and tests it contains.

The time has come to take flight financially and take the right steps to get out of debt and live in abundance.

Happy reading!

Teddy Ngbanda

Senior Church Pastor and Elder
Impact Centre Chrétien Bénin

INTRODUCTION

Why a book on "Getting out of Bad Debt"?

HOW TO GET OUT OF BAD DEBT?

The evil of debt and the uncomfortable situations associated with it are a reality almost everywhere in the world. Current statistics show that only about 10% of the world's population owns 76% of wealth and receives 52% of the income[1]. Apart from this supposedly wealthy fringe, which is supposed to be spared from debt (although this hypothesis has yet to be verified, as history and statistics have shown that the richest people are often the most indebted), 90% of the world's population is poor and crumbling under the weight of debt.

This is a serious and worrying situation, far more so than the coronavirus, malaria, AIDS, sex or any of the other challenges that humans are called upon to face during their time on earth. But it remains a taboo. It is very rare to see people together - even couples - sharing everything, without them sharing and trying to find ways out of their debt problems. And yet it's easy to see everywhere, in books, on television, on the radio and even on social networks, practical advice on how to succeed at this or that other thing in life.

When I was inspired to write this book on debt, I had fun looking for advice on how to get out of personal debt. I almost didn't find any, or at least I wasn't able to get any French-language document or tool dealing with the issue.

Vocational training schools including finance and management schools do not devote a single chapter to it in their curricula, nor do leading business! And yet,

---

[1] Read the World Inequality Lab's Global Inequality Report 2022 prepared by ANDREW STANLEY of the F&D team, March 2022.

teachers, parents, people of all ages, men and women and even students are faced with debt. Worse still, there are no awareness-raising campaigns on this scourge, which is slowly killing more people than AIDS, Covid19 and malaria combined.

Although it must be acknowledged that some people in the United States have taken an interest in the issue, very few French authors have written about it. Most of these authors and coaches confine themselves to guiding people towards financial freedom without treating the existing problem. As a result, no significant results emerge because they are content to develop misunderstood theories.

Working at a major university in my country, which is full of tenured professors who have produced research results in a number of fields, as well as senior lecturers in management and economics, I was confronted with the harsh reality that no research had yet been carried out on this issue. And yet it is a truly worrying subject. There lies the evil!

It's a very real scourge. Today, nine out of ten people are in debt. Since no one is immune, it is more than necessary, indeed essential, to talk about the evil of debt in order to identify and publicize ways of eradicating it from the face of the earth.

The aim of this book is to shed light on an area that has remained dark for thousands of years. It is intended to be practical and to raise awareness about the daily behaviours to be avoided in order to encourage a change of attitude for a brighter future.

Far from being a collection of theories developed by researchers without any significant contribution or result, this book is a guide based on proven and tested behaviours and practices. If you decide to apply them, you will see a radical transformation in the way you manage your personal finances.

Bonne lecture!

Chapter 1

MAKING A DIFFERENCE BETWEEN BAD AND GOOD DEBT

To make the distinction between bad and good debts, I will define these two concepts using two common illustrations that we tend to overlook every day. I will relate them to you here to give you a better understanding of these two concepts.

First illustration

"My friend Willy took out a loan of $80 to temporarily escape pressure from his landlord to pay his rent of $60. This was at a monthly interest rate of 15%, with the deposit of his computer, worth $200, as collateral. The loan contract clearly stipulates that his computer is considered to have been sold to the creditor if he doesn't bring the money in after one month".

Does this situation seem trivial to you? But it's true. You'll tell me that you can't or won't solve your problems by resorting to a loan shark. Let me ask you this: Have you ever run out of top-up to make a very urgent call and had to borrow credit from your mobile phone operator? If you have managed to do this once, you have done a lot worse than my friend, because this loan from your operator is often repayable the same day or a few days later. But the operator gives it to you with an interest rate of 10% for the day or three that you go without recharging your phone.

Someone will claim that it's just 20 cents or $1 worth of credit, that he or she doesn't lend beyond this amount. But the worm is in the fruit. You have just done more than my friend Willy, because in all cases, you took this loan to solve a very urgent or serious problem. In his case, he took a loan with a monthly interest rate of 15% whereas you wouldn't wait a single week to repay a loan at 10% interest. Sometimes you take out the loan so that you have enough credit to apply for a larger loan.

Second illustration

I read the story of funeral expenses, told by Ricardo KANIEMA in his book *La chèvre de ma mère (My mother's goat)*. It simply sickened me.

In this story, a father who had just tragically lost his child still had to face enormous expenses to move the family from the village to the city for several days for the funerals. The example he set at his own wedding was also truly bizarre. I highly recommend this very informative book.

What follows is a case similar to situations described and experienced in Africa for burial ceremonies or repeated celebrations.

'To bury their mother in style, Mr Claude and his elder brother urgently put up for sale a piece of land inherited from their grandmother. And as you probably know, in property transactions, when the buyer knows it's urgent, he sets all the conditions that suit him. To avoid being shamed at their late mother's funeral, they were forced to lower the price of the plot to $1,500, even though it was already worth $1,800 in the area concerned. Despite this, no potential buyer showed up until Thursday, on the eve of the burial, when they called on a mutual friend.

Taking stock of the situation and getting to know the area, Mr Gilbert, the two brothers' friend, was immediately interested in their offer. Unfortunately, he didn't have a penny to his name, as he was also in debt. When he forcibly applied for a loan of $1,600 (usually, loans with a minimum monthly interest rate of 10%), his lender initially refused, arguing that the year was already closed and that he had stopped granting loans as it was time for him to recover current or outstanding debts. But after much pleading, he finally agreed to grant the loan at 5% interest over two weeks.'

On this condition from the lender, Mr Gilbert managed to get the sellers to pay 5%, i.e. $80. The plot, which should have cost him $1,800, ended up costing him $1,400. He took advantage of the $250 to complete the land formalities, and two or three weeks later paid back the $1,750 to the lender.

Today, his property is valued at $5,000.

THE REAL QUESTION

Which of the first or second illustration was a good debt or a bad debt? In both cases, debts were contracted at a monthly interest rate.

Let me take you to an interview given by American entrepreneur and investor Robert Kiyosaki to a journalist on good and bad debt. In it, he explains how he and his wife Kim got out of bad debt. But first, he explains what good and bad debt mean.

'There are often two types of debt: good and bad.

- If I buy a house or a car on credit and have to pay for it with income other than that from the goods purchased, that's a bad debt. In other words, if I buy an asset on credit and that asset cannot enable me to repay the loan, then I have incurred a bad debt.

When I take out a loan to build or buy a house and I can't get any income from that house or car to pay my creditors, then my debt is bad.

A good debt is one that someone else pays for you or in your place.

But the reason this difference is so important to us is that it's easier to get into debt. In other words, it's often easier to get loans on consumer goods than on commercial property or to build a house to rent out or even to finance your studies. So, it's important to keep investing and try to eliminate those bad debts by paying them off one by one, so that you end up with good debts.'

Banks generally offer more consumer credit than investment credit. There is more advertising for festive loans than for loans to invest in a business. What's more, the conditions for obtaining a party loan are more flexible and the funds are made available more quickly than any other credit.

All you need to obtain a holiday loan is proof of a regular income. But to finance your studies or business, you need to produce a lot of documents, including a business plan, as well as guarantees, endorsements and so on.

Can you see how it's easier to take on a bad debt than a good one? Society is organized to get us into debt. The case of Western society is even more palpable because credit is free and without many conditions. You can buy anything on credit, including cars and groceries. You can have everything even if you have no money. This is probably why these countries are said to be rich but heavily in debt.

How can you say that someone is rich but heavily in debt? How can you say that the world's leading economic power is the most indebted? Surely its citizens are heavily indebted too. In some African countries, it's quite common to see people knocking office doors offering items on credit, payable at regular intervals. Do you see how much of a craze we have for goods on credit? Meanwhile, it's not so easy to get credit to start a business.

This prompts me to ask you to think deeply: "What is this 'good' thing that does no harm and is so easy and available to acquire? Does your banker love you so much that he wants you to have a good time by offering you credit? How can something good be so easy to get?" It is useless to say that it's always through pain that you get something good. But I would like to point out the proportion in which consumer credit is easier to obtain than investment credit.

Personally, I think that anything you can easily buy on credit is bad for you. It can give you temporary satisfaction while damaging your finances. Easily accessible credit is detrimental to either your health or your finances, or both. No banker or credit institution, let alone the seller of any item, loves you enough to sell you credit if they don't know you can't afford to pay it back.

Simply compare the procedure for obtaining credit from a loan shark or financial institution with that for obtaining credit from a bank. The procedure with a loan shark takes almost no time at all. You can obtain credit on the same day if you provide a cheque and some papers showing your movable and/or immovable property. The procedure with a credit institution, other than a bank, takes a little longer and is less restrictive. But the procedure at the bank is very restrictive. When the bank tells you the conditions, especially for young entrepreneurs, you feel like leaving the business.

How do you explain this situation? Do you think loan sharks and microfinance institutions like you more than banks? Absolutely not!

The cost of debt, i.e. the annual interest rate with a loan shark, is at least 100%, whereas microfinance is around 20 to 25%. Banks will lend you around 10 to 12% a year at most.

So, if you take out a loan of ten million francs with a loan shark, you will pay twenty million at the end of the year in capital and interest - the cases shown in the first and second illustrations speak for themselves. The same loan will cost you at most twelve million, five hundred thousand from a microfinance institution, whereas the bank will only take eleven million, two hundred thousand from you for the year.

Where do you think it's easy to get credit? Which creditor is hurting you or your finances the most? The loan shark, isn't it? By lending you money, it's the loan shark who gets the extra interest that wipes out your savings. Because if you can use all your income to pay off your debts, your suppliers (water and electricity companies, landlords, taxis, restaurants, etc.) will applaud you every time.

The truth is that there is a global system in place to increase individual debt and, in turn, global debt. The system is set up to promote debt so that no one can easily decide where their resources should go.

In short, a good debt is simply a debt that makes you rich and that someone else pays for you, like your tenants who pay you monthly rent, while a bad debt is a debt that you have to pay and that makes you poorer every month.

Increase your financial intelligence

When it comes to financial education or coaching, a lot of people just say, 'get out of debt', and that's a good idea if it's a bad debt. However, if you want to be a smart investor or have a high financial Intelligence Quotient (IQ), it's important to realise that there is such a thing as good debt, and that's what I've explained in the previous paragraphs.

Intelligence is knowing how to use debt to get rich faster. This brings us to our next development, which is how to distinguish between good and bad investments, between investment and consumption expenditure and between good and bad debt, so that you can get out of bad debt.

DISTINCTION BETWEEN GOOD AND BAD DEBT?

What generally distinguishes good debt from bad debt is that good debt will increase in value over time if you take it on; whereas bad debt will often depreciate and not increase in value over time if you take it on to buy goods.

So, what is a good debt?

A good debt is a debt that you take on and that someone else repays or pays off for you. For example, the rent paid by tenants on a loan taken out to build the house they rent. At the end of the loan term, not only will the house revert to the owner, but it will also increase his assets. The owner will then begin to enjoy the benefits of the rental income.

The same applies to a loan taken out to buy a bus for public transport. It's the same when you take out a loan to buy a plot of land. In the long term, you will benefit because sooner or later the plot of land will be worth more than you paid for it.

A good debt is a loan you take out that will generate future income or something that will increase in value. When the banks look at your creditworthiness and see that you are making regular payments, you will have no problem taking out a new loan in the future.

SOME EXAMPLES OF GOOD DEBT

Now that you know what good debt is, let's look at a few examples of loans that are considered to be good debts.

1- Taking out a mortgage to build or buy your main residence

A loan to buy your principal residence is a good example of good debt because it is considered an investment and should increase in value over time.

When you rent a property for twenty or thirty years, for example, hoping that your situation will change or improve before you build or buy your main residence, you have just made down payments on the property without owning it at the end of the twenty or thirty years. When you pay $85, $125 or even $170 to your landlord over thirty years, you will have capitalised, without interest, the minimum sum of $30,000. And if, over the same period, a friend were to take out a mortgage of $25,000 to build a three-room house of the same size and even larger than the house you live in, at the end of thirty years he would have repaid - with a monthly payment of $85 - the sum and would keep his house, which would no longer have the same value as the sum originally lent.

After thirty years, it makes more sense for you to build your house on credit than to pay the rent over thirty years. It's true that $30,000 isn't enough to buy a main residence, but rent doesn't cost 20 cents either. Decent accommodation in France, depending on the city, would cost at least five hundred euros a month, and in Africa, tens if not hundreds of thousands, depending on the country and the city.

Comparative studies depending on your geographical location are available on the Internet. I've also discovered an Excel spreadsheet that allows you to make simulations based not only on your country's tax, property and financial regulations, but also on your income and the monthly payment you are able to make. You can download it from the link below[2] and if you don't quite understand how to use it, write to me at hubertcea@gmail.com and I'll help you to define the most appropriate model for you.

I personally experienced this when I bought a plot of land on credit. I bought it with the help of a brother in June 2014 for $3,500 on credit from a property developer, with regular monthly payments of $33 for eight years. Even though the plot wasn't worth $3,500 in 2014, by May 2021, when I had finished paying off the loan, the price of the plot in the area was between $4,000. In other words, had I accepted the retirement plan proposed by life insurance companies or by banks, on this date, my savings would have amounted to $400 - at an interest rate of 4%.

Having chosen to buy a property instead of a pension plan, on the same monthly payment, I made a profit margin of between $500 and $1,300 over eight years. Personally, I think that apart from covering unforeseeable risks, it would be better to invest in property rather than opt for a pension plan.

I know that the question of building your home with your first income is debated at length by personal finance experts. But here I'm comparing long-term rent with a mortgage for a principal residence, which is very advantageous over time.

If I have to pay $85 or $115 a month to my landlord for thirty years without getting anything in return, I'd rather borrow $25,000, repayable over the same number of years, and end up with a house worth a bit more. If you're not financially astute,

---

[2] https://www.bibliosansfrontieres.be/ressources/feuilles-de-calcul-khan-academy/

I'd advise you to get out of renting as soon as possible. That will help you in the long run!

Nevertheless, you need to choose the best rate for your mortgage. This is a good alternative. Instead of paying rent every month, owning a home allows you to build up a mortgage that you can use in the future.

In addition, the value of real estate and property tends to appreciate over time, and mortgages generally carry very low interest rates.

Finally, as this is usually a long-term loan that can last for years, it allows you to arrange payments at a relatively low level, freeing up your money to make other profitable investments or pay off previous debts.

2- Taking out a mortgage to invest in property

In the investment jargon, leverage is the use of various financial instruments or borrowed capital to buy a new asset with the aim of achieving a return on investment.

In the property sector, the simplest example of leverage is a mortgage, which essentially involves using debt to buy property or, in other words, using money to buy income-producing assets that are likely to appreciate in value. Taking out a loan of one hundred and fifty thousand euros, for example, building rental leases constitutes leverage.

3- Financing your studies with a student loan or financing your children's studies on credit

This is a common practice in the West. Although repaying a student loan can be painful as a recent graduate, you can at least console yourself with the fact that it is considered good debt. That's because it's a way of helping you to prepare for and have a better career, a higher earning potential and to earn more money.

If President Obama hadn't had credits to finance his education, he probably wouldn't be in a position to steer the destiny of the world's leading power. At the end of your last semester, think straight about planning a monthly repayment system, because the sooner you start paying, the less chance you'll have of turning it into a bad debt.

4- Acquiring a business asset on credit

As a general rule, banks and financial institutions lend money for the acquisition of assets based on a company's business concept.

As a reminder, a 'business asset' is an item that forms part of a company's assets and whose expenses can be deducted from tax.

The difference between a business asset and a fixed asset is that a business asset is an element of your company's assets represented by fixed assets. By definition, a fixed asset is an asset intended to be used for several years of business activity, with an acquisition value in excess of a certain amount, depending on the regulations in each country.

This asset is likely to lose value over time, either because it deteriorates with use or simply because it becomes obsolete. The handling of this phenomenon in accounting is called depreciation.

Assets that must be included in your business assets

These are assets acquired specifically for use in your business. You must record them in your fixed assets journal and on the depreciation schedule. This category includes, for example:

- customer introduction rights or integration rights;
- equipment and tools specific to your business;
- assets acquired under finance leases;

- shares in companies that you hold in a non-trading company, a professional partnership or a stock brokering company, etc.;
- shares in healthcare establishments, provided that they are a requirement for your practice in said establishment.

You may decide to immobilise other items that are less specific to your profession. These may be assets such as a car or premises. Keeping a car in your private assets may have certain advantages, for example. Allocating an asset to your business assets is not an irrevocable decision. You can decide at any time to transfer it to your private assets and vice versa.

Why allocate an item to your business assets?

If you allocate an asset to your business assets, you can deduct all related acquisition and use costs. On the other hand, you will be subject to business capital gains tax if you sell the asset, cease trading or return it to your private assets (unless you are exempt under specific conditions).

If you do not assign the asset to your business assets, you can only deduct the running costs (maintenance, repairs, etc.). You cannot, therefore, deduct loan interest, property tax or other charges relating to the ownership of the property.

In short, a business asset is a fixed asset in your company's assets. You can deduct the related expenses from your tax bill and assess its real value over the years. While some assets must be depreciated, others can be included in your private assets and either leased to your company or used on a lump-sum basis. So, it's up to you to consider the best option for your business, but don't panic. Your chartered accountant is also available to support you! However, the assets you wish to assign to your business assets must be items that will increase in value and not depreciate over the years.

Bad debt is the opposite of good debt

Bad debt, as we mentioned earlier, is debt that is easy to take on and can be damaging, as it forces us to pay it off on our own by looking for money elsewhere, outside of what the original loan enabled us to acquire. If you borrow money to bury a relative and there is not enough financial support to repay it, then you are forced to use your salary or other income to do so. This reduces your assets and your financial leeway for looking after your children or family. Similarly, if you buy your personal car on credit, it certainly gives you comfort and coverage for your family members, but you have to create a new expense line in your income to pay it off.

A bad debt is the opposite of a good debt and has the following characteristics:

- is considered a non-essential debt. Its interest rate is often high;
- does not generate income over the long term;
- is a debt that has been generated to buy things that will quickly lose their value;
- may be a good debt that has not been settled or that has been passed on to a collection agency.

If you take out a loan to buy something that will depreciate quickly or that you cannot repay in full (which will result in further additional costs), this is a bad debt.

Examples include a purchase made with a shop credit card or consumer credit, in other words any unnecessary purchase.

SOME EXAMPLES OF BAD DEBT

a) Borrowing money for a relative's funeral

These situations will be discussed at length in this book, as they are common in African society. It is best to avoid taking out a loan for your parents' funeral expenses. It doesn't help! The death of a parent already causes pain, so will you add the pain of debt? This is by no means a good sign for your financial future and that of your family. Jesus told one of His disciples to let the dead bury the dead. In some regions, there are practices that seem absurd, more so when they are carried out with debt. It really isn't the best option to honour the memory of an illustrious departed.

b) Borrowing money for the end-of-year party

The party is usually celebrated over a period of two or three days at most. Party loans are repayable over ten months. Can you imagine taking out a five-day loan that deprives you of the full benefit of your income for ten months and then, a month later, another party comes along? Are you going to borrow again? Will you spend your life borrowing to celebrate? It becomes a vicious cycle for some people. Please get out of it!

c) Buying non-essential luxury goods on credit

Most people consider buying a car to be a necessity. I won't suggest otherwise in this book, especially when you live in the countryside where it's becoming increasingly difficult to get around without a car. However, you should be aware that from the moment you drive it, it will automatically lose value. For that reason, you should avoid going into debt wherever possible. Buying a new luxury car with a loan of $33,000, for example, is a frivolous purchase if you can't afford it. This is an example of bad debt.

d) Useless consumer credit

Before discussing consumer credit, it is important to talk about consumer goods. A consumer good is a good that does not produce positive cash flow. In other words, it does not generate income, neither for its own upkeep nor even for its owner. Consumer credit is therefore money borrowed to finance consumer goods. Let's assume, for example, that you buy a new motorbike showroom on credit for $1,700, with an interest rate of 10% monthly payment, or a loan for the end-of-year party. If you only make the minimum monthly payment (which is around 10% of the balance) of $180, it will take you more than ten months to pay it off! At the end of these months, the showroom will no longer be worth its original price, and you will have paid more than the showroom is actually worth. This is the case for most of the latest items, which lose their value over time and are replaced by more recent models.

Chapter 2

SOURCES OF BAD DEBT

There's a myriad of sources of bad debt. There are so many things we could mention, but we will concentrate on those that we know and have experienced, through personal experience or through our friends and relatives.

1- Elections in West Africa

Electoral events in my country, Benin, are often tantamount to considerable expenditure. It's a time when the balance of power in financial matters becomes apparent. Here and there we hear that presidential campaigns cost tens of thousands of dollars. From personal knowledge and the testimony of close relatives, the electoral expenses to be elected as a municipal councillor at district level vary between $25,000 and $70,000, depending on the district, to run an effective campaign.

Campaign accounts may prove me wrong, even if I am aware that these accounts are not always drawn up on the smallest scale of municipal elections. The response of a candidate friend speaks volumes: 'It's a big deal, isn't it? It depends on the environment and the political context. I run the central borough and I'm up against the outgoing Mayor. So, it's not easy. But all in all, I must spend about $33,000. But I wouldn't advise you to be a candidate. You can support, finance or play a leading role. But being a candidate is another matter. I don't know what your situation is', he told me.

For a young employee with ten years' experience in public service who wants to be a candidate in such a campaign, where will he find such financial resources? No doubt he would have to take out loans or sell his property. I remember that my friend offered me one of his plots of land in the centre of the country to cover election expenses. But how much property could a young man, be he a civil servant or an entrepreneur, already own? Absolutely not enough! So borrowing is the real source of funding for these elections, and the end result is a delicate financial situation.

I have relatives who, after an election campaign, have never seen each other again. Fortunately, in Benin, this practice is on the way out thanks to the recent law on the party system.

2- Large-scale demonstrations

The stories told by Ricardo Kaniema in his book *'La chèvre de ma mère'* (My Mother's Goat) about his wedding and the burial of an army officer's child are vivid testimonies to the practice of pompous festivities in Africa. Once again, I recommend that you read this book.

2-1 High-profile weddings

Ceremonies marking the transition from singlehood to married life are major occasions of expenditure for newlyweds, especially young men. And given that people are getting married at a younger age, some brides and grooms do not yet have sufficient means to cope with the many demands of wedding ceremonies. From the dowry to the nuptial blessing, there are considerable expenses involved. So, most people take out loans to meet these expenses. After the festivities, such loans become heavy debts that the newlyweds must face in addition to the needs that come with life together.

I really appreciated my older brother's behaviour when he wanted to get married. At the time, he confided in me that he wouldn't have any financial difficulties after his wedding. To achieve this, he invested $3,500 in an operation while he was in the middle of organising his wedding. Few Africans have the capacity to do that.

Fearing that he would be broke after the wedding festivities, he invested two million of his savings in a market gardening business. At the end of the festivities, the simple fact of seeing young carrot plants, lettuce, tomatoes, onions, peppers, etc. grow was a sign of hope and joy in his heart.

2-2 Burials

There's no point in talking about what the loss of our dear relatives costs us in Africa. It's not a question of what the death of the person causes in our lives, but rather of what their departure from this world costs us.

And since we can neither plan nor contemplate the loss of a loved one in the same way as a wedding or an election campaign, funeral ceremonies are times of great stress and unexpected expense. Naturally, you have to ask for loans from family and friends, or even from your own salary. Once the ceremonies are over, you are often faced with debt situations that require long-term management.

3- Lack of knowledge in a business area

Most people have never learned to manage their money properly. Moreover, they don't try to acquire the knowledge they need to do things properly. They simply perpetuate the same habits from generation to generation, hoping that one day things will change. If you don't ask yourself how the industry you're in works, if you don't feel the need to understand the rules of the business you're in, you risk making mistakes and ending up in debt.

4- Lack of planning and discipline

Many people spend impulsively because they have no plans or budget to ensure that their spending does not exceed their income. The lack of discipline and planning in your personal budget can lead to unmanageable situations. Failure to plan leads to unwise choices and lack of discipline leads you to mismanage your income. This increases your expenditure and leads you into debt.

5- Unexpected circumstances

Sometimes in life, unforeseen situations arise that require unexpected spending. In these cases, people get into debt when they go through unexpected events such as illness, an accident, a fire, the loss of a job, and so on. Although these are urgent situations, sometimes amounting to life-or-death matters, the fact remains that money you borrow without having a source of income to plan its repayment is bad debt. We've all been in this kind of situation at least once. Learn how to set aside a budget in your income to deal with unforeseen situations.

6- Shareholdings at the start of local tontines

In Africa, it is common practice for people to build up their savings by getting together in groups of ten, twenty, thirty or even five people, to make contributions that can be collected in turn. This method allows people to put money aside in a collaborative and supportive way. These are known as 'grouped tontines'.

These opportunities present serious difficulties for the first recipients of these tontine shares. For lack of knowledge or financial savvy, it is common to buy consumer goods using these resources, forcing ourselves to pay each instalment from our salaries or various parallel incomes.

This is a source of debt that compromises relationships and creates many other uncomfortable problems. I have a sister who stopped going to church because of a badly managed tontine. Sometimes years of friendship are shattered in a matter of minutes because of these situations.

7- Building a home or buying a car

Buying a car can be done with your own money when it's well planned, or with a loan when it's impulsive or suddenly urgent. A personal vehicle may be urgent or suddenly important out of conformity or necessity. In the latter case, the rapid arrival of a new baby a few months after the wedding, or even the wedding itself, can lead young couples to acquire a vehicle to get around. Added to this is the cost of fueling and maintaining the car, which makes it difficult to repay the loan on time.

Building your own home, from acquisition of the plot to completion, can cost an average of between $33,000 and $50,000, depending on the area chosen and the amenities required for the construction or fitting-out of the building. If it's not well planned - which is often the case - it becomes a source of debt that can be carried for a long time.

3- Bankruptcy in a business

Bankruptcy is the inability of a company to honour its commitments, and when it occurs in a business, it becomes a source of debt. The shareholders and/or directors of a company that defaults on payment may find themselves faced with heavy debts to manage over the long term, resulting from ill-considered decisions or circumstances beyond their control. These are just some of the sources of debt that I have been able to identify.

What other sources of debt have you come across? Answer truthfully and resolve to discipline yourself to improve the quality of your personal finances.

Chapter 3

ARE YOU IN DEBT?

NINE QUESTIONS

TO FIND OUT

To find out whether you are in debt, I encourage you to do a test that I was once led to do during a workshop on finances run by my faith leader, Pastor Teddy Ngbanda. So, please put your book aside and grab a sheet of paper and a pen. We will be answering "Yes" or "No" to nine questions in a row and then continue the reading adventure.

Are you ready? I really must insist that you grab a sheet of paper and a pen, otherwise I confess that you won't need to continue reading this book, because understanding what happens next depends on it.

So, for Question 1, answer "Yes" or "No" depending on the answer that speaks to your current reality, not the reality you experienced in the past nor the one you expect or hope to experience when you have a lot of money.

Be true to yourself. No one must see your sheet at the moment. It's a personal exercise, more confidential than the results of your tests at the hospital or your confession to your spiritual father. This is between you and God alone. Therefore, there's no need to lie to yourself or to God.

Note: Write each number with its letters on your sheet of paper and tick "Yes" or "No" according to your answer to the corresponding question.

So, looking at your current situation:

1- Are you in the habit of paying your bills late?

a- Are you in the habit of not paying your bills on time?

b- Do you usually pay your water, electricity or post office bills by the due date?

c- Do you pay your rent or your employees' wages on time?

d- Do you respect the deadlines you give to your friends and creditors every time you borrow their money?

2- Have you ever hidden a bill from your spouse or fiancé, parent or brother? yes or no?

a- Have you ever hidden from your husband/wife/fiancé(e) the bill for a purchase that you made without their knowledge and that you are having difficulty paying?

In Africa, it's difficult to understand the concept of an invoice. The invoice is linked to any purchase that has been made but not yet paid.

b- Have you bought fabric, shoes, earrings, ointment, underwear, clothes, watches, kitchen utensils, etc. without your spouse's knowledge and for which the creditor keeps asking you to pay?

3- Have you ever let a breakdown on your car or motorbike drag on because you don't yet have the money to repair it? yes or no?

Or if you don't have a car or motorbike yet, maybe it's something useful like your spoilt or broken television that you've left lying around. By way of illustration, I have a sister whose bed base broke, and it took her brother's return from school for the Easter holidays before she saw the bed repaired. Is there anything you use that you've let drag on for repairs? Your household gas refill, your old chair or your children's study table that doesn't fit any more, your sofa torn somewhere, etc.? Tick Yes or No as appropriate.

4- Have you bought anything recently that you didn't need and couldn't afford? yes or no?

This question is simple and clear.

5- Do you frequently spend more than you earn? yes or no?

Does what you earn sometimes not allow you to finish the month before you have another income? Do you manage to finance your basic needs and those of your family normally until your next salary? If not, you are spending more than you earn.

6- Have you been refused a loan recently? Have you applied for a loan from a private individual (friend, brother) or from the bank? yes or no?

Has your bank or credit institution, your creditor, your friend or even a member of your family refused you a loan recently when you were seriously in need?

7- Do you gamble or engage in sports betting to get out of debt? yes or no?

Do you hope to win the lottery to get out of debt?

8- Have you ever used up your savings (if you have any) because of hard financial times? yes or no?

Have you ever used your savings for a party, your children's schooling, the funeral of a loved one, your children's birthday or christening?

9- Do your total debts (excluding property debts, if any) exceed your total savings?

If you do a little sum in your head, could what you have in your accounts be enough to pay off all your debts?

Summary

Count or calculate the number of 'yes' and 'no' responses you have received.

There are four possible statistics:

- either you have only Nos

- or you have only Yesses

- or you have more Yesses than Nos

- or you have more Nos than Yesses.

If you only have Nos, *bravo!* You have complete control over your finances. If you only have Nos, then you probably don't earn any money yet. You don't have any income yet, and here again, you should take a very close look. I doubt you have ever borrowed money from your mobile phone operator for an emergency, if only to call your parents or guardian to tell them that the car or motorbike has broken down or is on the way, or to ask for help if you run out of petrol.

If this is the case, it's much easier to answer No. But if such is not the case, you don't need to read this book... Yet, I invite you to read it to realise how good you are already, unconsciously. It will give you more confidence and strengthen your relationship with money.

If you have between 1 and 5 Yes scores, it means that you need to make adjustments to reduce bad debts;

If you have between 6 and 9 Yes scores, I'd ask you to be careful because you are heading for financial disaster;

If you have only Yesses, then your financial situation is very critical and you will need to change your behaviour and attitudes quickly, otherwise you'll be jeopardising the future of your children and your family. I encourage you to continue reading this book, which gives you tips and advice on how to improve your financial situation.

I'd like to remind you that it's important to be honest with yourself, because it's difficult to solve or cure a problem if you don't have a clear picture of the whole thing. Introspection is necessary to gain full awareness and make the right choices to free yourself from debt and save your financial future.

The Bible, the most widely read book in the world, does not say that borrowing is a sin, but it strongly advises against it. A debt is money or goods that one person has to pay back to another. This includes money borrowed from banks, friends, family, credit card companies and financial institutions.

Regarding debt, the Bible tells us not to owe anyone anything except love (***Romans 13:8***). It therefore advises against owing our neighbours money or possessions. This is understandable because debt is considered a form of slavery. We read in

Proverbs 22:7 that '***The rich rule over the poor, and the borrower is slave to the lender.***'

Even Muslim law or the Koran provides for deprivation of freedom for debtors; in other words, if you owe someone money and don't pay it back, you can be imprisoned or your relatives can be used as slaves to extinguish the debt. We do not have full freedom to decide where we will spend our income if we are obliged to repay a debt.

Finally, I can say that debt is a curse for those who disobey. If the Bible advises against it and we do it, then we are disobeying God's Word. God has warned us several times about disobeying His Word: *"But if you do not obey the voice of the Lord your God .... **the sojourner who is among you shall rise higher and higher** above you, and you shall come down lower and lower. He shall lend to you, and you shall not lend to him. He shall be the head, and you shall be the tail."* ***(Deuteronomy 28: 43-44)***

Chapter 4

THE CONSEQUENCES

OF

BAD DEBT

It is important to get out of bad debt because your inner and outer peace of mind depends on it. If you find ways to escape from your creditor, know that he too is looking for ways to keep you.

Sound advice

I have two colleagues, Grégoire and Ichola, with whom I have friendly relationships. It often happens that I owe them money, to either, or even to both at the same time. I often owe Grégoire and almost all the time Ichola because the latter doesn't claim his debt. He leaves me until I feel embarrassed about the length of the debt, or when I feel it will affect our relationship, I pay him back. Ichola is inclined to lend in this way to almost all his friends without always coming into possession of his money.

Grégoire, however, is very generous in lending you what you need, but it's important that you set a timetable and stick to it. With five days to go, he starts writing to you to remind you of what you owe. The same day, at 9 o'clock in the morning, he'll write or call to let you know that he's waiting for you to sign. I found him annoying and despised him, not knowing that he was obeying one of his principles: "If someone owes you money, write to them every morning at 8.30, if only to ask about their family". This was the advice he gave Ichola when the latter complained about his debtors not honouring their words and commitments to him.

When Ichola started to put this advice into practice, he began to receive payment schedules for debts dating back two years or more. And indeed, the more he continued with the morning greetings, the more he collected.

Debtors, be aware that creditors are actively looking for ways to deal with your situation. They've decided to undermine your morale every morning because when I saw Grégoire's call every morning, I lost all control. So, you should know that the creditors have decided to sabotage your day for as long as you continue to owe them.

Creditors make you lose your day

Your day is your main asset for moving forward. The best way not to let creditors spoil your day is paying off your debts. Imagine that every morning at 8.30 a.m. for the past month you have been receiving calls or messages from the same person you owe. You have just lost a month to build yourself up or to perform well in your field of work.

Imagine you're praying and your mobile rings, or you're with your boss, colleague, partner, child or wife talking about a serious problem. How would you feel? I'm sure that your self-esteem and enthusiasm would drop and, above all, you'd lose your head in a split second. Imagine if you were at a job interview or negotiating table right now!

Debt makes you lose your inner peace

Debt takes away your peace of mind. In fact, when you owe someone money, you often don't feel at peace when you see them. Some people think so much about their debts that they develop psychosomatic illnesses. Blood pressure problems here, heart problems there and the daily worries that go with them. You really need to make a plan to pay off your debts to regain your inner peace.

Debt reduces your credibility

You should be aware that your debt situation reduces your credibility with potential partners. The other strategy my friend Grégoire used to make me pay him was to inform our mutual friend Ichola. As I said earlier, these are my two friends who regularly come to my aid when I need them, and besides, Ichola lends me money without counting the cost and without pressure. So Grégoire's other trick was to inform Ichola that I'm not paying him what I owe him. Yet I owed Ichola $1,700 before Grégoire's debt was incurred.

What would your attitude have been at that point? I think that if you loved yourself and were concerned about your financial future, you would quickly honour your commitments to these two friends. So, remember that the more you develop strategies to get out of debt or make your creditors forget about it, the more they too will develop strategies to recover their funds, even if it means disturbing your peace and disturbing your mental health.

Similarly, in my quest to collect my debts with a client, I obliged him to issue me cheques on a regular basis. Aware that my debtor was unable to honour his commitments because he had nothing in his checking account, I obliged the bank by means of a bailiff's writ to record my debtor's insolvency. This led the bank to cancel the credit availability procedure initiated by my debtor with the bank. As a result, my debtor lost the confidence of his bank.

Do you know how far insolvency can take you? These examples can come in many forms to discredit you in the eyes of your business partners. You'll tell me that there isn't a single bank out there. Let me tell you that if you don't resolutely decide to get out of debt, the debt situation will end up with you jeopardising your whole life. You'll find that over time people who were initially willing to listen to you and give you any support, even if it wasn't financial, will no longer respond to you as attentively. As a result, you will lose credibility and trust.

Debt leads to disrespect

At the time, my debtor's insolvency led me to disrespect his most loving wife, because I knew that the more I touched him where it hurt him most, the quicker he would pay me back what he owed me. When we take out a loan, we often have good intentions and are prepared to meet all the conditions demanded by our partner. We are led to show the good side of our lives. This is how my debtor showed me around his oil palm field and his wife's restaurant, which was familiar to one of my best friends. Knowing his insolvency diminishes his reputation with all these people, my debtor felt obliged to pay me back.

Just because someone owes you money doesn't mean you should feel superior by using it as an excuse to ridicule them and make them lose their dignity. I'm sharing these past experiences here to show you just how destructive debt can be to the relationships (professional, friendly, business, etc.) you've taken years to build.

Debt stresses and increases loss of stability

How would you feel if you unexpectedly met your creditor in the same environment as you? Especially as he called you three days ago about his money and you didn't pick up? Imagine you've been invited to an oral presentation and your creditor is in the audience, in the front row right before you. Inevitably, you will be disappointed and will try much harder to keep your cool and get out of it.

Debt mortgages the future

Debt reduces your room for manoeuvre. When you have expenses to cover and have to meet your commitments, it may be necessary to defer or postpone meeting certain needs until your next income or for the future. From deferment to deferment, you are concentrating on needs that are necessary for the future.

How long have you been putting off financing additional training in your field of activity? How long has it been since you took the time to spend a weekend with your wife and children, just to strengthen family ties? Or to rekindle the love and feelings you shared twenty years ago? Finally, when would you like to send your child to some language immersion programme in some English-speaking country? This has been going on for years now.

Complete this list yourself according to the reality you are going through. Take stock, become aware and make resolutions to change the situation.

Debt leads to poor family upkeep

Indeed, this needs no further proof. When you're in debt, it's the members of your small family who suffer the first consequences. All the little calculations and sacrifices fall on the family. The upkeep you need, the learning you need, the environment you need for your family, all take a hit because of your financial situation. I think your family deserves better than the treatment you're giving them because of these damned debts.

Chapter 5

SUPERFICIAL FIXES TO DEBT

Politics has never put an end to the money problem because it does not teach us how to generate residual income, i.e. create wealth. The income generated can be enormous in a short space of time if it works. But it only works for those who have learned how to create wealth. So, when income is plentiful, they start channelling it into profitable assets (especially plots of land). More can be done!

Political positions and benefits are often spontaneous and high above our way of life. For example, when someone receives political promotion, their status changes. They get a new car, a driver, petrol vouchers and a bit more allowance. All this changes their lifestyle, so that without a clear plan and vision, most of the money they collect is spent on trivia and expenses. They will no longer be able to buy food in the usual places; they will have to buy new clothes and so on. In the space of three months, the new agent obtains a new social position which is unfortunately not sustainable (at most three years for the luckiest).

For elected positions (MPs, mayors, presidents), you fall into ruin the last time you fail to turn up for the elections. A relative of mine invested over $50,000 of his savings to campaign for the position of mayor. He finished his savings to the point of borrowing nearly $8,500 more. Imagine if he lost these elections when he was already retired and hadn't learned how to create wealth!

Politics is not a way out of debt. Moreover, failure in an election plunges candidates into an unmanageable debt situation. You only have to look around you at the lifestyle of politicians at the end of their office term to see this. So, avoid going into politics to solve your financial problems. You can't dig your way out of a hole. If you aspire to politics, review your motivations and prepare yourself so as not to sink if you fail.

Cutting expenditure

Another solution to the debt crisis is to cut spending. The truth is that we are not really cutting spending. As I said, you defer the need. Otherwise, a need remains a need as long as it is necessary for you and your family. Cutting expenditure only leads to putting yourself in uncomfortable situations, unless that expenditure was timely, necessary or useful. If not, by how much can you reduce your monthly budget for transport, restaurants, meals at home or your children's schooling? You can reduce your expenditure, but not by so much as to solve your debt problem. You can perhaps reduce the number of clothes or shoes you buy yourself every six or eight months, but it's not significant. You can reduce the number of times you go out to eat, but it's not obvious because you'll be eating anyway. Reducing these monthly expenses will not fundamentally get you out of debt.

Selling your cow to pay off liabilities

Another mistake people make is trying to sell their assets to pay off debts incurred to buy assets that are liabilities. For example, taking money from one's capital or business to pay a tontine received to buy a motorbike or to have a party. This example is trivial. We don't notice it, but we do it every day without realising it. Using your business or your capital to pay off a loan to buy a personal vehicle or to pay off work done on your main residence is one of the sudden solutions to debt.

Selling a source of income is not the best way to solve your debt problems. You can sell assets that don't generate money, such as fabrics, shoes, bags, television sets, etc. The cow is like your capital or your property. She is like your capital or your investment or your land. Just as it produces milk and calves for you, your land can not only increase in value, but you can also earn income from its cultivation. You can also earn a salary and a dividend from your business. So don't sell your cow to pay off debt, or you'll run out of wages and dividends.

Looking for qualifications to obtain promotions and enjoy a golden retirement

At the start of my university education, I was impressed by most of my teachers, only to be disappointed by some of them when I was hired to work there. I really admired the teachers at the university when they each came to give their classes. And because it was a vocational school, we knew a lot of teachers who not only made us love their subject, but also their lives. I enjoyed seeing these professionals come and teach us about their profession. Sometimes they would tell us about their lives outside work, and that made me particularly keen to become like them. But a few years after my graduation, when I was recruited to serve as a financier at the same university, I was surprised by some of the realities of the teaching trade to the point where I no longer wanted to become a teacher.

I was lucky enough to be taught by a highly qualified and experienced professor, a university lecturer, a member of a very high-level constitutional institution that had his own research laboratory and won contracts for economic research. This man was full of life, spreading terror in the classroom and showing a good standard of living. I'm sure that many of my fellow students were also impressed, except that they didn't see what I was lucky enough to see afterwards.

Five years later, I found myself in a position where I had to serve many of the teachers who had looked after me during my studies. One day during a conversation in my office, this confession by one of them terrified me: "I thought that with a pension of $500, I was going to get by. I can't even get around". When he left, I got down on my knees and asked my Lord never to put me in that situation again.

That conversation was the turning point in my life, by the way! Otherwise, I also thought I'd have a very good professional career by multiplying my diplomas and trying to teach at the university. But I didn't like knowing about this hidden phase of my teachers' lives. So, from this year 2014, I started researching what a good professional career means, what it is like to never run out of money again and I can assure you that it is neither in a professional career nor in the unbridled pursuit of degrees.

If diplomas gave money, the most highly educated people in our respective countries would be the richest. And experience shows that it's those who haven't run after qualifications who create wealth and recruit those who do.

I once knew a teacher who, even after going blind, continued to look for qualifications so that he would still have a bonus of two or three more years before retiring. This man, if he had $30 worth to collect from your accounting office, was prepared to wait a whole day for you to come and pay him. I noticed on several occasions that he would wait for me for pennies.

I knew another not insignificant person, who was owed $100 and whose file was not yet ready. He told me that if he didn't get the money that day, he wouldn't be able to go home because his child wouldn't be accepted in class the next day for lack of his training fees. I have another university lecturer who borrowed $9 from my accounting department as an advance on his fees. I had to pay for it myself.

If you are relying on degrees to get you out of debt and see your situation improve, I'm in a good position to tell you that you're mistaken. I spent nine years of my career serving the most highly qualified people in my country, who, in addition to being teachers, had held the highest offices in the Republic, and cumulatively so.

The aim is not to devalue long studies and research, but rather to promote motivation based on problem-solving and service to humanity through research findings.

For example, a doctoral thesis can cost its author between three and $6,000,000. How can a young person invest so much in research, obtain results and not even share them with society in exchange for something? And it's only when they've finished their doctoral thesis that they start looking for part-time teaching jobs!

Personally, I was tempted to do research that could lead to a doctorate, but when I realised that I couldn't use it immediately to solve my money problems, I decided to research the problems facing society. I have identified several scourges that I'm working on. Here is one of the products of my research in your hands. It makes me feel more useful to society and I systematically get a return on my investment, even more than I would be paid for thirty years of teaching.

Seeing people free of debt and seeing their personal finances grow is a great blessing for me. A person who knows how to manage their finances properly and who, instead of investing in useless consumer goods, learns how to create wealth can also get others out of similar situations. This satisfaction beyond anything is truly priceless. A degree doesn't make you rich, and neither does a job!

Multiplying working hours

Another mistake is trying to do several jobs. Just remember that even if you try to work a whole day without interruption, you can work fifteen to twenty hours a day at most. And even if you are paid $85 an hour, your income cannot exceed $4,000 a month. This may help you to deal with occasional situations and financial problems, but it is at the sacrifice of your health, your family and your extra-professional life.

Chapter 6

DOWN WITH PROCRASTINATION!

Procrastination is the tendency to put off until tomorrow things that we can do today. We have all been known to say "I'll do it later" to a task that we could have done straight away. If you are the type of person who always puts things off, you are simply procrastinating. And to put a stop to this phenomenon in your life, it's first important to discover yourself, to get to know yourself better in order to identify what might be causing it.

Practice is the best way to learn and get results

I followed a leading figure in business planning in a programme organised by my church, *Impact Centre Chrétien*. This programme, called 'Impact Finances', is often a three- to five-day programme during which eminent personalities who have succeeded following Bible principles interact. One of these personalities is particularly dear to my heart. It's Mr Jean Claude Tschipama, the former CEO of Eutelsat Africa and current Deputy Director of Equity Bank in the Democratic Republic of Congo.

During this seminar, Mr Tschipama developed the theme 'How to make a success of your professional career'. This leader proposed an essential exercise based on the discovery of our true identity. So, he asked us to write a precise 15-page document, Arial font, size 13, left and right margin about ourselves, who we are, our academic and professional background, our history and what parents, friends and family think of us.

Are you aware of who you are? This is the starting point in the process of success. The real question you need to ask yourself is: "Who am I really?" Are you aware of the talents you have, the potential buried within you? How many years of professional and work experience do you have? Are you a happy person? What factors allow you to say whether you are satisfied or not? If not, what are you missing?

To identify all these elements, you should devote forty (40) hours to in-depth personal reflection. Take out a 100-page notebook, or your computer or tablet and write down this reflection, describing your personal story. This will enable you to respond to this reflection in a detailed and authentic way. Ask yourself what you're passionate about, what motivates you every morning when you wake up. What keeps you awake? What are your areas of fear? Where are your anxieties and worries? These things will help you refine your thinking.

Next, what do your parents say about you: mum, dad, children, brothers and sisters, neighbours, your colleagues at work, your supervisor, your CEO, your pastor or your brothers in the department if you attend church.

Ask your children and your wife. Ask them how they find you. How can they describe you? Are you a tidy, dirty person? Are you meticulous or ambitious? This is an introspective exercise designed to make you aware of who you are. It's a vital step in finding out where you're going and what you can achieve. It enables you to lay the foundations for the crucial stages in your life and to draw up an action plan for the success of your professional life. It is your life story that is a crucial step in the process of your professional success, a step in determining the fundamental elements of your professional financial future. If you are interested in this exercise, do the exercise and join me on my page www.ayanouhubert.com or on one of my social network accounts.

To tell the truth, the exercise is very complicated, if not difficult to do. But Mr Tshipama added something surprising to the instructions. He said: "Do the exercise. If you don't, you are cursed". I followed the seminar offline, but when he said that, I must admit I was shocked, and I am sure more than ninety per cent of the participants in the room were too. To threaten people with a curse for an exercise that concerns their own lives, and this in the church that is supposed to deliver the faithful from the same evil, really shocked me. And that led me beyond shock to try to understand why he could make such a threat.

To tell the truth, this threat led me to do the exercise because I was also going through a period where I was looking for ways to develop professionally. I was going through a period of disgust. I had just spent more than five years in the same job and all my attempts to change jobs were in vain. Although I wanted to change jobs, I was determined not to accept just any offer, no matter how big or well-paid. I don't want to work in a similar position again, because my past experiences didn't give me a positive feeling. I'm now looking for a professional environment that suits me better.

The exercise enabled me to rediscover my spiritual and professional identity. I was able to know with conviction what my faith was based on and precisely the kind of job I could accept. It saved me a lot of unnecessary running around. Yes, I could no longer run around hoping that something would work out. I ran knowing exactly where I was going. I was no longer impressed by anything. At a time when my colleagues and friends were running to go into politics to win any position, I was serene because I knew exactly, thanks to Mr Tshipama's exercise and other tools, what suited me very well.

Confirmation of the threat

I read the response to Mr Tshipama's threat later in the book *'Increase your financial intelligence'* by Robert Kiyosaki in which he presented Edgar Dale's cone of learning. In the cone, the author shows the rate at which we assimilate everything we learn. He recommends that if we want to master a concept, we have to practise it. The more we practise or teach what we learn, the more we retain it. This simply means that if we commit ourselves to teaching or practising a concept, we have a 90% chance of retaining it or curing ourselves of it. But if we just read or listen, we retain no more than 10% of what is developed. And that's why we criticise our education system, because it's based on listening and reading with almost no practice. That's why we have students who have graduated brilliantly from vocational schools but are unable to meet the demands of the jobs for which they have been trained.

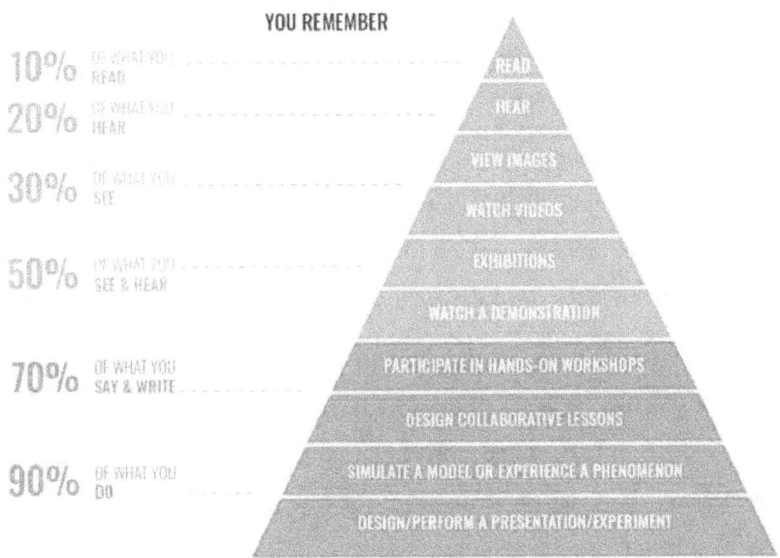

If you don't put into practice the concepts and advice I'm sharing with you in this book, you'll have wasted everything, including your time!

When I read this book by Robert Kiyosaki in which he presented the cone, I decided to put it into practice. In fact, reading it inspired me to apply IQ number 1 'To make more money'. It's an exercise in which the author recommends that we find our billion-dollar idea, i.e. the idea that can solve a global problem and whose solution will earn us billions. I thought long and hard to come up with an original idea. That's how I came across a passage in which the author gave ideas on how he and his wife got out of bad debt.

Strangely enough, I immediately started looking for the CD he mentioned. On Amazon, as on other sites, the CD was out of stock. I searched in vain for the

French versions. I called a friend in Germany who used to help me pay for a lot of things in Europe. He did some research but there were no books in French about bad debts. I then wrote to a friend in the USA, who had difficulty finding English versions of the two CDs. That's how I became convinced of the seriousness of this problem and of the darkness that awaits us if nobody talks about it.

I decided to specialise in this area, as I was going through a serious period of debt myself, linked to the building of my home. I bought books in English, which was an original idea for French-speaking folks. However, I found myself unable to find anyone to help me understand the content of the CDs and audio recordings. So, I set out to work.

I can assure you that at the end of the day, the result is there. As I had to write about it, I mastered it 90%. This got me out of debt, led me to write and share my experience to earn even more money by applying IQ number 1 and finally to become a personal finance training consultant.

Today, no matter how serious your financial problem, if you decide to follow the rules described here, you'll be pleasantly surprised by your performance after two years. If we stick to what is said above, you will have understood that simply reading the lines in this book will not get you out of bad debt. If this book doesn't tell you to change anything in your daily life, it will have lost all its meaning and usefulness.

So, if we've taken the trouble to write prescriptions, it's because we want this book to be a real tool for you to get out of debt. To this end, I recommend that you systematically put into practice what is said, otherwise you will have lost everything. You will have wasted your money by buying this book and you will have wasted your time reading it. You should have taken that time and money to treat yourself to a visit to the beach or the mountains to relieve your money problem just a little.

However, you will be called a cursed individual if you waste your time and money, because this attitude would be similar to that of a person diagnosed with cancer who was prescribed medication but, after buying it and reading the dosage, put it away in his drawer. If that's not a curse, maybe it's stupidity. And I wouldn't wish that on us. My only wish as I write this is that everyone who reads it will get out of debt and take flight towards financial independence to the benefit of their family and community.

I strongly recommend that you read Robert Kiyosaki's book *'Increase your financial intelligence'*. I read it interactively. Every time I came across a new concept, I took the time to research it on the Internet to understand it better. I have never read a book like it. It literally transformed me in several areas.

For example, the notion of developing multiple intelligence reoriented me in the way I supervised and monitored my children's schooling. I have realised that each child is unique and that we shouldn't expect them to be necessarily brilliant in the linguistic and logical-mathematical intelligence that is mainly encouraged in our schools. I am now convinced that I must support each of my children in the intelligence they develop, while helping them to develop other types of intelligence. This has led me to follow a number of training courses and to become a consultant in educational and career guidance. I have even changed my view of my wife's affairs.

A call for general awareness

When a company is in debt, it either closes down and declares itself bankrupt, or declares itself insolvent. The regional law governing companies in the West African Economic and Monetary Union (WAEMU) protects them against their creditors. It will be protected against everyone and given time to rebuild. If that still doesn't work, it will be liquidated and the creditors will only take a proportion of the after-sales proceeds of what it has left. Either another lessor may decide to buy the company, or the government may decide to support it, either by granting tax relief or by nationalising it.

When the State falls into deficit, it turns either to the central bank or to the primary banks, or it addresses itself directly (through bonds) or indirectly by receiving savings left in the bank or in social security funds.

And what about the average person, i.e. you and me? Who knows our debt situation? Nobody, except ourselves. No creditor bank understands you, not even the State, through local and central government, grants you tax relief. Your boss won't give you a pay rise. Even the charges won't wait for you. Your children's school fees, domestic and parental charges, contributions, car fuel, telephone bills, etc. do not give you any extenuating circumstances. You have no support from anyone. You are on your own! So, you need to take your financial life seriously, and not just play around with it.

Chapter 7

PRACTICAL ADVICE TO GET OUT OF BAD DEBT

Yes! We're on chapter seven! Congratulations on having read this book so far. I appreciate your determination to get out of bad debt and better manage your finances. And in this chapter, I share with you twelve (12) tips and tricks that will help you get there if you put them into practice. Many of them have been recommended by Robert KIYOZAKI and his wife Kim.

A. Commit your debt situation to God

'Commit your way to the Lord; trust in him, and he will act.' (**Psalms 37:5**)

'Cast your burden on the Lord, and he will sustain you; he will never permit the righteous to be moved.' (**Psalms 55:22**)

This first step will or may seem trivial, senseless or even pointless to many, but it is very important to me.

One of my favourite verses states, 'By faith we know that the universe was created by the word of God, so that what is seen was not made out of things that are visible.' (**Hebrews 11:3**)

Not everything we see in the world is made of things we can see. Whether the thing in our lives is material or immaterial, as long as it is of this world, it is first and foremost made of things that are invisible, and therefore spiritual. We therefore need to regulate its operation in the invisible before regulating it in the natural or physical world. Your debt situation is invisible before it appears in your life. If you're not convinced, there's no point in reading any further; otherwise, you'll simply have added another book to your reading list.

The aim of this book is not just to give you tips and techniques for getting out of debt. With your help, it aims to be a guide to dealing with your debt situation in a profound way, so that you are free of this challenge for good. So, we're going to tackle it from the inside out, from the invisible to the visible.

The first thing to do is to turn to God and tell Him about your situation. After all, didn't the Lord say: 'Do not be anxious about anything, but in everything let your *needs be made known to God in prayer and supplication with thanksgiving'? (**Philippians 4:6**)*

I think that getting out of bad debt is also a need like any other need for housing, travel, training, marriage, blessings, etc. So, make your debt situation known to God and ask Him to deliver you from it.

B. Be honest, tell yourself the truth!

There's a quote in my mother tongue that illustrates the idea that you can't hide your nudity in the shower jar. For the record, in Sub-Saharan Africa, it was often in a jar that water was supplied for bathing, even for drinking before the advent of tap water. This practice is still customary, as the jar is made in such a way that the water it contains is very cool and helps to combat heat. The water in the jar no longer needs to be put in the fridge.

To return to our subject, it is impossible to hide your nudity from the jar that contains the water for your bath and with which you will make yourself clean. It goes without saying that you have to strip down to the last item of clothing when you get into the shower for the bath.

This anecdote also applies to your financial life. When you want to be financially clean, it's essential to wash. Washing means undressing and getting naked, not hiding anything, because in the shower, it's you and you alone. The rest is just equipment.

Even if you finish bathing and get dressed up, as Ivorians say, only you know everything you've done before leaving. Even if you're hiding the latest bill from your partner or doing your best to conceal your financial difficulties from your children, you need to get into the shower to look at yourself or to see yourself face to face.

What's your current financial situation? How is it evolving? If nothing is done about it till the end of next year, three, five, ten years from now, what would happen? What will your creditors do with you if in 6 months, 1 year, 3 years, you are unable to repay them?

If you continue to accumulate debts, how will you be able to repay them? What are you counting on?

That other creditor you promised on the 15th of next month, when you are honestly not counting on anything, how do you expect to repay him? Your children's schooling, your mother-in-law's funeral debt, your child's christening on the horizon - you can't just bury your head in the sand and pretend nothing has happened.

Look at yourself and observe the situation. If possible, wake up when everyone else is asleep and take stock and make peace with yourself. Is it necessary for you to take the fabric from the funeral of your colleague's father-in-law, take fuel to travel and give out an envelope because he attended the funeral of your mother-in-law for which you had borrowed $850 that you had not yet repaid? Of course, the fabric, the sewing, the travel and the envelope don't add up to much. It's barely $50 and that's nothing compared to what you owe. Besides, if you don't attend the funeral, your parents are still alive and no one will come to their funeral, even though it's 'If you do me, I do you'. And if by chance there were five very close people who had ceremonies, could you sew the five fabrics, give out five envelopes and attend all five funerals that weekend?

If you have to attend all these funerals to honour your friends with your presence, and come home all tired when you're already working from Monday to Friday without a break, when will you have time for yourself to think about the crucial situations in your life, such as your debt situation and the strategies you need to implement to get out of it? It's true that invitations are opportunities for us in Africa to have fun and enjoy ourselves, but do we need to increase our debts to do so? $50 isn't a lot of money, but if you do it three times a month, that's $150. Are you sure this won't affect your commitments?

Do you have to buy phones every year? Does your current situation allow you to pay for the upkeep of a girlfriend? You might say that she doesn't cost you much... But if she makes you spend at least $35 a month (including credit, hotel room and pocket money), takes up your time (to greet her in the morning, to stay together with her to manage minor conflicts), my brother, with all this, how do you expect to get by?

Does Mademoiselle or Madame need to pick up the latest collection of new Vlisco or Dutch Wax fabrics? What's the point in you chasing after all the 'trendy girls' if your serious problems aren't solved? Do you need a private flat at this stage in your married life?

These are questions you need to ask yourself in order to examine your situation in detail. Telling myself the truth is, I think, one of the hardest things I have ever had to do. Prepare yourself accordingly because it's not going to be an easy thing to do. Once you have decided to face up to it, you will tell yourself the truth, the sincere truth that comes from the bottom of your heart. Tell yourself the truth about your debts. Face up to the harsh reality of them. Take stock of how much you owe and to whom. Hold yourself accountable for your debts and don't pretend you're financially well off.

Most people who make the mistake of pretending that everything is fine only make things worse. In fact, that's what leads them to keep accumulating new debts. So, it's always a good idea to be honest with yourself when it comes to debt.

C. Don't accumulate new debt

*'The prudent sees danger and hides himself, but the simple go on and suffer for it'. (**Proverbs 22:3**)*

Resolutions should emerge from the answers you find by confronting yourself.

Eliminate the debts of imitation that make you feel like keeping up with the Jones. Did you know that just because your friends are doing it doesn't mean you have to do it too? The exercise you did at point B, you did it alone because it's about your financial life, and your family's future, not friends' or colleagues'.

You need to make firm resolutions already on certain expenses. You can't damage your family's financial future just because you want to please your colleagues. There's nothing wrong with not sewing ceremonial fabrics. Your friend or colleague may need your presence or even just your financial support. Send them an envelope or agree to go as a group to reduce travel costs. You can support him or her with half or even all of the travel costs and fabrics, and still have time to reflect and work on an essential issue in your life. Talk it over with your partner. It's hard to do, but you have to do it.

Today, no one in my family is angry with me because I didn't buy the fabrics for the festivities. Sometimes, they send me an invitation adding that I don't have to attend, and at least they hope I will turn up. What are you afraid of? Are you sure that if you don't go from one funeral site to another, nobody will attend your parents' funeral? Not even the people in the neighbourhood where the ceremony is taking place? And even if no one did come, what's the real embarrassment?

Personally, I have chosen to celebrate life rather than death. In fact, my absence from funerals and other events allowed me to use my weekends and public holidays to work on things that contribute to my personal and professional development. To write this book, I had to set aside some time. It wouldn't have been possible if I hadn't decided to set my priorities aside from my day-to-day activities, rather than responding to all the requests.

No one will kill you for not buying the latest fabric with the new pattern. You don't need to waste the rest of your day escorting little girls to bars and hotel rooms. Instead, spend it with your family or strategising about your financial future.

This means you may have to make a few sacrifices:

Cut back on spending and live on the essentials

- Talk to your family to find a balance that won't put you in a difficult situation today. Your family is important, so it's essential to communicate and reach a consensus.
- Do you need three or four cars of your own to spend money on every month? What if you sold one or two of them to pay off some of your debt or invest the money in a low-income activity? At least you won't be spending on several cars at once.
- There was a time when I couldn't afford to buy new shirts, socks or trousers. I would use the ones I had a little longer and do my best to keep them clean and tidy. Some people don't know how to live on the bare minimum while they rebuild themselves financially. You have to learn to adapt to each season of your life because you are only accountable to yourself.

I have been criticised several times by both my family and my friends. All I could console myself with was that I was the only one who really knew where I stood financially. I was also the only one to decide whether or not to get out of it, and the same goes for you. It's not up to your friends or family to decide, it's up to you. Once you're back on your feet, the money will start coming in a little more regularly. But during this period, make it a point of honour not to waste your money on things that will only put you further into debt. Define and complete your budget and avoid any unforeseen events destabilising it as much as possible. Once you have taken responsibility for all your debts, put an end to any new debts. Close your spending circle and don't allow the slightest unforeseen event to upset your budget. It's true that during the month, you're bound to come across unforeseen, life-saving situations such as your car or motorbike breaking down, or one of your parents or even your children falling ill. Create a line in your budget for the unexpected. It takes discipline, courage and dedication, but above all don't forget that it's a process. The transition from where you are now to where you want to be won't happen overnight. And if you don't have the dedication, courage and discipline, this process, not because it's a bad one, but because of a lack of determination, will have no remarkable success in your life.

D. Make a list of all your current debts

Which brings us to the next step, which is to make a list of all the debts you have. The key word here is EVERYTHING!

Don't get me wrong when I say the word 'everything'. Even if it's a mountain of debt, it's only by eliminating it one by one that you can finish off. And if you don't make a list of all your debts, you won't be able to draw up a good plan for paying them off. This step is vital and indispensable for the rest of the process.

Even if you don't remember everything, put a notebook beside it and for a month write down the names of your creditors every time you remember them or see them on the road or elsewhere. Take the time to draw up an exhaustive list of your debts. With your Android, you can create this list and add to it wherever you are.

Spend this time with your partner if you're married

If you're married or in a long-term relationship, you probably know that you need to go through this process with your partner. If you choose to join forces for life, your debts will become your partner's debts too. It would therefore be a good idea for him/her to be aware of your previous debts.

In any case, I know that you didn't get married just for the sake of happiness, but to grow together. You will become smarter together, you will understand each other better because the process from debt to wealth is a great journey and it will make you love each other more.

There are also many women who just want to hand over all the financial responsibilities to their husband or partner. I don't recommend this because the most important thing in this whole process is what you will learn together. Oh yes, you are going to learn a huge amount together about your mistakes, and the strategies and ways that it takes to get money. It really is a process of growth.

Couples break up over difficult and complicated money issues. Here's an opportunity for you, as a couple, to grow together by solving a really big problem, which is getting out of debt and getting rich.

Make decisions

After making this list, determine your current financial situation. Then decide whether you should sell some of your possessions to reduce your debts.

Your assets include your possessions, your goods of whatever kind, and your liabilities represent your financial charges. Once you have worked out the difference between your assets and liabilities, you can decide whether there are any of your assets that you could sell to reduce your debts. See if it's possible to part with a few suits, jewellery, dresses, cars, houses, plots of land and so on to ease the pressure on you from your creditors.

E. Keep your spirits high, forgive yourself and restore your confidence!

Keeping your spirits high is the most difficult thing after the debt inventory stage. Whatever the size of the debt, you need to keep your spirits high to deal with it. Otherwise, faced with the total amount of all these debts, you will be tempted to run away or do anything, but this is the time to be serene. It's no coincidence that you have this book in your hands.

It's possible that once you have finished taking stock, you will be overcome by fear. You may wonder how it all happened and whether you can get through it. Let me tell you that YES, you will get through this! I have heard of people committing suicide over a trivial debt of three or seven million and others running away from their environment. This kind of behaviour doesn't allow you to solve the problem or make it go away.

Face the situation, forgive yourself and decide to put an end to it by implementing the plan described here. You will be surprised to see that day by day you gain confidence and carry on with your business. What's more, you will be able to develop new activities and eventually see the debt disappear completely.

I liked one brother's attitude to his debt situation. He was going through a period where every time he got credit to finance a deal that was promised to be profitable, he ended up with a shortfall of twice the amount borrowed, and ended up with even more debt to pay. This went on and on, and his debt increased each time he executed a deal, until he ended up with a debt of over a hundred million or even ten times that amount. Then he had the foresight to realise that this situation, far from being visible, was first and foremost spiritual. With the help of his financial partner, he stopped operating, took stock, learned from the situation, dealt with the problem correctly and spiritually before starting his business again.

F. Use a written plan to control your cash inflows and outflows

This phase is crucial for anyone who wants to get by financially. It will ensure that your expenses do not exceed your income and also identify any surplus money that can be used to pay off certain debts quickly.

This is a vital, if not very important, step in creating a monthly budget and controlling what comes in and what goes out.

I started this exercise in 2017. Before the start of the year, I defined my budget and before the start of each month, I prepared my monthly budget. Every time a sum fell into my hands or into my accounts, whatever its origin, I automatically recorded it. Every time I had to part with a penny, I had to record it immediately.

At the end of the year, I aggregated the budgets executed over the twelve months to get an idea of everything that had come in and everything that had gone out of my pocket during the year. I was amazed in the first year of this practice to see what I had earned in one year. I could never have imagined that I could handle so many resources in just one year. I did some soul-searching to see what concrete or tangible things I'd been able to achieve with these funds. Nothing concrete. I went through the broad outlines of the expenditure budget, and noticed that it was nothing but consumer spending. I sat in front of the computer for almost an hour thinking about how I'd been wasting money since 2011 when I started earning income.

This exercise is great. I recommend you start now even if you're not on the cusp of a new year. This will help you prepare for the next year so that you can manage it better than in previous years.

For my part, I took the annual budget template from Microsoft Excel and adapted it to the different income and expenditure lines. At first, it was a bit rough. But year in year out I improved it and today I have a good tool for monitoring my budget. I later took some excellent workshops on personal finance and discovered some powerful personal finance management tools. I invite you to get hold of this excellent tool by Pastor Christian Saboukoulou. Try to adapt it to your cash inflows and outflows, and if you can't figure out how to use it, write to me and I'll help you.

So, with a budget drawn up and properly monitored, you will have an idea of your different sources of income. From which activity do you derive most of your income? From your salary, side activities, donations? If you have several activities, now is the time to create a line for each of them. This will enable you to see at the end of the year which activity has brought in the most and what changes need to be made to the others.

In my revenue lines, there was a source of income with which I began to feel less and less in tune with myself. I no longer had peace of mind when I earned money from this source. And yet it represented almost 60-70% of my annual income. At the end of 2019, I sighed and prayed that I would no longer earn money from this source and at the beginning of 2020, my professional situation changed and this source was automatically cut off. But my annual income didn't change.

In both 2019 and 2020, my income was practically the same. Which is to say that when you are not ready to make changes in your life, you can't see that there's a better situation than the one you are in and that you like it there. Today, I earn practically the same as I did in 2019 and I have peace of mind. So, thanks to this change, I have gained in serenity.

Similarly, after a year, I can easily tell you how much I have spent on repairing my car or how much fuel I have added to my car. This exercise enabled me to see, for example, that my first car cost me $1,734 in 2019 for its maintenance and various repairs, excluding fuel. This led me to realise that my car, which I bought at the end of 2014, had become too expensive to repair and I sold it at a residual value of $1,700. I then took another, more comfortable car, which in 2020 cost me $650 to maintain.

I could also read that, in 2019, my consumer credit expenditure was $400 compared with $750 in 2020. This can be explained by the fact that during the Covid-19 pandemic, everything moved online. So, I invested in a modem that I recharged to the tune of $40 every month so that I can take part in training courses and attend services online.

I also noticed that in 2019, I spent $786 in restaurants compared with $820 in 2020. This has led me to reduce, for example, paying for my friends every time we get together or every time I come to see them at our dining place. The strategy is to only get out of my car with what I need to pay my bill. I prefer to act in this way to avoid any additional expenses due to my impulsiveness. I am aware of my impulsive tendencies and that's why I take this precaution.

The day I made my close friends aware of the need to have a monthly budget and stick to it, I shared with them the cost of my hair care in 2019 to motivate them. They burst out laughing saying that I'm really not serious because the amount was estimated at $24. They asked me how I could account for all the money I spent in the hairdressing salon.

I assure you that this exercise is fascinating and will lead you to reconsider certain ways of spending. For example, in 2019 I invested $850 in training and buying books for my culture and personal development, compared with $950 in 2020. I can now see why the desire to write was born because I have received a lot and it is obvious that I am emptying myself to receive more. My way of sharing is to write, because my personality test shows that I am introverted and that I will find it hard to captivate and hold an audience's attention during my training and self-motivation courses.

On the other hand, the same test proves that I have talent for writing and that I will be more fulfilled in tasks where I am focused and turned in on myself. I understood all this during the training courses and tests I took. So, the $850 I invest in myself every year will enable me to get to know myself better and become increasingly knowledgeable in many more areas than those in which I already earn money. Isn't that interesting?

Do you know how much you spend in bars each week? How much do your extra-familial relationships cost? Do you have any idea? I am in possession of some personal knowledge that I prefer to keep confidential for the time being. That's why every day and every year I am improving my financial, professional and personal life. And what about you? What's your plan for personal and financial growth?

I paid off 3,950,000 CFA francs of debt in 2020. I didn't notice that I paid off any debts in 2019. Of the $6,500, there's $4,700 that I convinced my uncle to give me to compete with my resources to open a money transfer business - Western Union, MoneyGram, Mobile Money, etc. and other activities -. Unfortunately, the brother to whom I entrusted the business, who had in the meantime come to ask me for a job to help him get by, embezzled the money.

This situation almost led to a dispute with my uncle, but I was able to repay the money. This is to tell you that in your debts, there are things that come directly from you and situations created by those close to you or your entrepreneurial initiatives. This brother's attitude is strange. I promise to come back to this experience in detail in my next book on the art of controlling your investments. At the time when I was handling the day-to-day activities, this gentleman was responsible for managing the small business for eighteen months without producing any reliable results. When the time came to call him to account, he started avoiding my questions, creating conflict situations that were difficult to manage, both in Cotonou and with his family in the village.

Just to show you how controlling your income and expenditure can help you plan how much you can repay each year. And when you go through the lines of your budget carefully, you will see that you will find the unnecessary lines that will increase your ability to repay.

G. Making a budget and sticking to it is an important key.

How do you keep your accounts and manage your budget?

In my experience of financial education, there's one fundamental point that professionals in the sector regularly remind us of: keeping your accounts. As the years have gone by, I have tried out all the existing techniques for managing a budget and my conclusion is simple: there is no perfect technique, each one has its own particular characteristics.

Doing your accounts is the cornerstone of personal finance for the simple reason that without forecasting your budget and managing the inflows and outflows, you can't implement any plan: you're limited to a monthly view, the only one that can be mastered effortlessly.

A few years ago, I was introduced to managing my accounts using the good old-fashioned method: the notebook in which I wrote down my expenses and the monthly statements sent by my bank. Was it fun? No! And I didn't manage to make it a lasting habit.

Since then, a number of interesting techniques have come to light and, as my budget is much more flexible, I have opted for a lighter way of doing things without spending several hours a month doing my accounts. You will discover a few simple techniques to apply, but don't forget that managing your budget is essential. If you end the year broke, that's not a good sign. Only the State or a start-up that has raised funds can afford this kind of folly. If you have any plans whatsoever, for example to go on holiday next summer, you need to do your accounts one way or the other to find out whether this is possible or how it might be possible. The ultimate goal is to make sure that the start of the new school year doesn't put a strain on your budget by the time you get back from holiday.

The techniques for doing your accounts are simple. As with everything, it's crucial to understand the reason (why you should do your accounts) rather than focusing solely on the manner and techniques, as the saying goes: *'If you want to do something, find a reason; if you don't want to do anything, find an excuse'*. Basically, doing your accounts is very simple: it involves plotting out your income and expenditure and planning a budget for the year, and especially on the eve of each month.

If you are one of those people who live as if their income is unlimited, you are outside the scope of this book. For the rest of us, having a budget is a good thing for one reason only: to plan ahead and be serene.

The envelope technique

The envelope technique is slightly different. To use it, you need to draw up a provisional budget. The easiest way to do this is to monitor your spending over the course of a month (even if there are sometimes quarterly or other expenses) and then work out how much you need to spend.

For each category of expenditure (food, leisure, transport, subscriptions, tax), the idea is to withdraw the money in cash at the beginning of the month and put it in a specific envelope: this will be the budget for the month for that category.

The tricky thing about this technique is that it puts the finger on all the little expenses that blow up the budget. This can be unpleasant and perceived as a 'Yes, you're living beyond your means, you poor coward!' thing. It requires discipline: don't go back to the cash machine when the envelope is empty halfway into the month. In any case, if your budget is tight, this is an excellent technique for regaining control. You can combine it with the first one and set aside some amount for your savings first, which makes the system worthwhile. As the months go by, you will be able to anticipate exceptional expenses and control your budget by knowing by how much you should reduce your spending in each category.

The ant technique

Ants like to count. They works hard to save. I don't know many people who practise this technique and I have to say it scares me! Likewise, if you are an ant, you may already be practising this technique and if you are not one, then it will scare you. Be that as it may, the ant technique is ultimate budget control. It involves, as I have been doing since 2017, tracking every expense and pointing to your bank statements. Where most people scan their statements looking for an abnormal transaction, the ant points precisely to each transaction. The advantage is that nothing escapes it, but the downside is of course that all this takes time.

The ant technique is perfect for controlling your spending and creating, but above all following, a precise budget. If you are a basket case and want to become the king of budgeting, this is the best solution available. This technique enabled me to quickly detect irregularities in the management of an activity entrusted to one of my brothers. He was spending money on himself without remembering that the business was not his property, confusing the company's resources with his own pockets. That same year, his spending spree increased tenfold. He bought a car, organised grandiose masses on the fifth anniversary of his mother's death in Côte d'Ivoire and in Benin. He helped his wife get a degree, followed by numerous birthday parties. Subsequently, he became incapable of accounting for his management, polluting fraternal, business and friendship relations. He justified his attitude by saying that he had become too busy during the week and that, at weekends, invitations to various ceremonies meant he couldn't make a point of it.

If you don't get into the habit of counting, you can be sure that it will catch up with you.

H. Pay yourself first and define how much of the rest you want to spend paying your expenses and paying off your debts.

I first heard about 'paying yourself first' in 2014 at a workshop on finance. I must admit that many of us in attendance heard of this principle for the first time. It's a very simple concept, yet difficult to put into practice. The idea stems from the fact that when we receive our income, our first reflex is often to pay our bills (rent, electricity, water, children's canteen, transport, meals, telephone, etc.). Two to five days later, the money is gone. Where has the money gone? In the pockets of the landlord, the electricity/water company, the school and children's canteen, etc.

Paying yourself first means using your income first. In other words, the first thing to do when you receive your money or salary is to deduct the sums you wish to save or invest, of course after tithing if you are a Christian. That's all there is to it! The idea of paying yourself first is to ensure that we don't let everything that comes into our hands slip away and that we keep something to build our financial future. So, we must include ourselves in the expenditure lines and put ourselves in first place, because we have worked to earn this income. As a result, we need to hold on to something, not after we have got the essentials out of the way, but first. To begin with, you need to retain 30% of your income, broken down as follows: 10% for tithing, 10% for building your financial empire and 10% for your various short- and medium-term needs. I will come back to tithing in the last chapter.

I have a system whereby I always pay myself first. And if you read personal finance books, they will tell you ten per cent, twenty per cent or thirty per cent: one for savings, one for investment and one for tithing.

This means that if you earn $170, you pay yourself $50 straight away. Most people scream, hesitate, stop, cry and give up at that point. I mentioned at the outset that this is a simple concept yet difficult to implement, because it may be too painful to pay yourself 30% of your net income. So, start with a piggy bank. I don't care if it's one or ten cents a day, but get into the habit of remembering.

If you learn to put money aside for savings, investment and tithing, it will become a habit for you. And for those of you who have read Robert Kiyoshaki's *'Rich Father, Poor Father'*, you will understand that it's not money that makes you rich, it's your habits that do. So even when you are broke or in debt, you must pay yourself first. And the reason many people are probably still broke is that they never pay themselves first and just pay all the bills. In the end, they don't pay everyone off and they don't keep anything for their future either.

One thing is certain: even if you spend 100% of your income, it will never be enough to solve all your monthly problems - there will always be some left over. As Jesus said to Judah, you will always have the poor with you. So don't be one of those people who refuse to sow, invest or save by looking at their daily problems. Money problems will never end. Even if you earn $33,500 a month and have no investment plan, the money will slip through your fingers every month.

You will have problems every month. You can't pay for everything this month, regardless of your income. And since there will always be expenses to plan for, it's better to keep some of it for your future than to leave it all in the hands of others with no certainty of results. This is the only real opportunity to create a future that is different from your present. If you look at your current situation, you will do nothing. Ten years later, you will still be going through problems.

The rule is that you should get into the habit of setting aside 30% of every penny that comes into your household. It doesn't have to be 30%, but start with 10% or 20%.

When I suggested this to a couple I knew (both employed and in debt), this was their reply: 'We have ALL these bills to pay to ALL these creditors who are shouting at us. We are going to manage these bills first, and then we will put what's left in the banks.' And I'll tell you, that's why you are still poor and in debt. Make a point of implementing Law 30-70 even if you are covered in debt.

I'd like you to remember this: the most important thing after hiring someone is to apply the principle of paying yourself first. The reality is that only the poor and the middle class pay themselves last. Which class do you want to belong to? The rich, right? Do as they do. Behave as they do when it comes to money. If they have an income, it doesn't all go immediately into spending on consumer goods and leisure activities, let alone paying creditors. They keep some for needs and investments. Start now to pay yourself first, even if it means paying others with what's left over.

The hardest thing is to get off the ground, and if you don't have that 30%, assuming it's $17 a month, at least get into the habit of doing that, then pay your bills and you'll be surprised at how clever you are. If you must pay those bills because your piggy banks aren't screaming at you, people who want their money will. If you pay yourself first, the people yelling at you kind of give you the motivation to go out and get more money.

I'm always amazed at how quickly this money accumulates, because you say: 'It's forbidden to touch it, it's for investment, for charity and for savings so we don't touch it', but it accumulates quickly and can help you start something without borrowing. Only then can you finance your first property, a business without borrowing.

I have a friend with whom I attended the workshop mentioned in Chapter 3. Towards the end, the trainer asked and recommended that we immediately start to save only a tiny portion of our income. He told us not to allow our income to end up in our hands or in our accounts, without having set anything aside.

On the next Monday, my friend went to see his banker to issue a standing order to transfer money into his salary account: in other words, every time his salary was transferred into his account, part of it was systematically deducted and sent to his savings account. Although this attitude was difficult, it enabled him to start saving while continuing to pay off his debts. The simple fact of seeing these savings grow month after month, for his future, filled him with joy and confidence.

If you look and listen to most people who are really rich, they say: 'Save 50%'. John Templeton says: Putting 30% aside is pretty hard now, but if you work at it, you'll manage to put 50% aside and then increase it quickly enough that 50% will go up to 60%, then 70%. So today, even though I earn thousands of dollars in income, I'm investing around 40% and 60% simply because I have developed good habits during this process of making out good and bad debts. One of the reasons you can get rich faster today is by learning to invest.'

You can have a nice house, fancy cars and all the things you need to live that kind of life, but you just need to get into the habit of paying yourself first every time you come in. 30% will soon grow to 80%, and I think that's one of the biggest secrets to a successful remuneration policy.

Don't be like my friend who pays his bills first. I used my bill collectors and people who hated me as motivation to go out and earn more money, but I still paid myself first. That's my advice to you.

The other objection I often hear is 'I have no money to invest'. By reading this book to the end, you will discover the formula for paying off all your debts. You will also learn from this process how to pay off all your debts, and what's more, how to have money to invest if you decide to put everything it says into practice.

For this process to work for you, you need discipline, determination and stamina to see the gradual change in your financial life. If you follow this formula correctly after ten years, I think you will be happy with yourself and you won't be stressed after any job.

What I like about this technique is that it's ultra-simple. If you can't take out 30% of your income at the beginning of the month, then you're spending too much of your income. Although this method has its advantages, it's not flawless. For example, it does not allow for absolute precision when making decisions about the allocation of financial resources. Plus, you need to draw up a supplementary budget to determine how to allocate the available money wisely.

Paying yourself first is not really a technique for doing your accounts, but I have been using it for years and it has worked very well. It will work for you if you have a big margin between your expenses and your income, but wouldn't work for you if you have tight budgets that need to track your spending more precisely. When I have taken everything I wanted from my income, I can freely spend everything else without any remorse: my future is then secure.

To achieve this, set up a standing order for a transfer from your salary account to an account to which you don't have easy, direct access. You can decide later what to do with these savings as soon as the opportunities arise.

I. Talk to your creditors.

This can be before or after the previous point – it's up to you to decide what works best for you. Have open communication with your current lenders and try to find a solution with them. This can be difficult with some creditors, but I strongly suggest that you communicate openly and be honest with them about your situation. In fact, most of them are willing to work with debtors who want to repay their debt. Do this regularly and stick to your plan.

You should also describe the circumstances in which the debt situation arose and what led to your bankruptcy and/or the seizure of your assets. These could be circumstances such as a medical problem, loss of employment, something that will really help you if you have evidence that you went in and tried to resolve the problem.

After bankruptcy or foreclosure, when you are back trying to get loans, these kinds of things that you have already done will help you regain the trust of your partners. Some of them may be touched by what you have done, if it's sincere, and will support you in your efforts to put things right.

You must show them that you are trying to work with them to solve the problem, whether it's a two-way street or not; it doesn't really matter but you tried and it was a way out. Also, I think by discussing with credit advisors, you will keep their recommendations and act on them. Try to do what you can, even if you are going through a very difficult financial period.

I'm often asked, 'Do you have to be debt-free before you invest? My answer is 'No'! It's a choice you can make, by opting to invest even if you still have a few bad debts. You have to decide what's best for you. You don't need to finish paying off your debts to start investing. Create two lines in your budget. When dividing your monthly expenses by your income, consider the two lines as expenses, even though the investment will earn you money.

While you are going through this process, don't forget to make small investments. This is what will guarantee your financial future, not the repayment of debts. Paying off debt takes the pressure and stress off you and frees you up, but it doesn't give you a better future. The aim is not to pay off your debts and go broke, but to free yourself from them and take financial flight. Don't stop investing because it was part of the process anyway, so you develop the culture of investing even with little capital. Don't forget that the Bible advises us not to neglect weak beginnings.
- You need money to earn money, to keep on living and to pay off your debts.

J. Draw up a repayment plan for each debt and stick to it!

Get a visual image of each debt. To do this, simply draw a table with four columns. And in the top left-hand corner of the table column, you put the creditor. For example, this could be the school the children attend. In the top left-hand column, you will find the total amount due, the total balance due.

In the top right-hand corner, you will put the number of months it will take you to finish paying this debt. In the bottom left-hand corner, you will find the minimum amount you have to pay each month, and in the right-hand corner, you will find the outstanding amount.

In the bottom right-hand corner, you will divide your total amount due into payments.

Here's a template:

Creditor: Children's school

Total amount due:	Number of months:
Minimum amount to be paid each month:	Outstanding amount:

If you take, for example, a tontine of 20 people where each member contributes $85 each month, you realise that you have just lent $1,600 to 19 people, who will repay their share each month.

Creditor: Tontine

Total amount due: $1,600	Number of months: 19
Minimum amount to be paid each month: $85	Total amount due: $1,600

For each debt you have, you will create this visual or an Excel file with workbooks for each creditor. You will create another sheet or workbook summarising everything. This gives you in real time the general trend in the status of your debt.

If you are not computer-literate, you can use a large-format notebook for this purpose, or even your smartphone can help. It's up to you to find the most suitable tool for you. Do the same for other debts such as school loans, car loans, personal loans and so on. Even if you don't yet have a monthly plan, write down the names of everyone you owe money. In this list, also include your home, whether you own a house you paid for or built on credit, in which you live. Many people see their home as an asset, but in reality it can be a financial liability. With this process, you will become completely debt-free, including from your house and cars, if you follow it step by step. Yes, step by step.

Start with the smallest amount of debt you have. It's true that some people think it makes sense to pay the highest interest rate on their debt first. However, this doesn't take all factors into consideration. Sometimes, it may be more advantageous to prioritise the repayment of other debts, depending on the pressure the creditor is putting on you or the impact the interest is having on your finances. Every situation is unique, and it's essential to examine all the elements before making a decision.

In the process we are talking about, you want to get started, to see a result quickly. You want to know that this formula works. So, we will take your shortest debt, the one you can pay off the fastest, and when you see the result and its fruits, you will be able to see that the formula I am proposing works. This victory will encourage you to move forward. The reason for starting with the smallest debts is explained in more detail in the penultimate chapter. You will notice that it's not a large sum, and it's often interest-free. It's not a big deal. It's the quickest you can delete immediately. So, go through the list of all the debts and look at the circled number and put them in order from smallest to largest, and that's the order in which you will pay these debts.

No. 1 could be the amount owed the lady in the shop next door. No. 2 could be the loan from a colleague or friend, No. 3 the children's school fees and so on. Once you have all the numbers lined up, you move on to the next step.

Each month, put $17, $35, $90 or $180 aside. And if you say to yourself 'Oh, how can I find an extra, additional income of $17, $35, $90 or $180? I've run out, so far, I can't make any more money. What do I do?' Look in your monthly budget to find out if there are no unnecessary or less urgent expenses or lines than the creditors that annoy you every day. You are sure to find something you can cut and put towards paying off that debt.

The other alternative is to start small businesses. These will help you not only to round off the end of the month, but also to find extra money to pay off your debts. This is where you will see the importance of paying yourself first. Start a business with the 10% set aside for investment. If it's not enough to get you started in the first month, wait until the second month and get started. Not only will you learn with small amounts of money, but you will also develop an entrepreneurial habit that will enable you to learn and become smarter and smarter.

Small activities at the beginning don't need a lot of money, just your own involvement, time and intellect. It can be something other than a business, like the Internet package you take to follow training courses on YouTube or a book you buy in an area you're passionate about. This is the time to develop your hidden talents. The things you have been dreaming about but which time or financial resources have prevented you from achieving, such as small seminars for ten people. These days, you can do it online with your Internet package so that people can follow you from home. You can also start with biscuits and sweets in your workplace or tissue paper. These are low-capital investments that people need on a regular basis, or selling communication credits.

You can become an estate agent or broker by using these small savings to pay a professional and make your social accounts visible through advertisements. You can also use your savings to travel to negotiate virtual sales contracts with suppliers. The transactions that come out of your posts can generate commissions many times higher than your salary. Imagine receiving commission on a property deal worth a hundred million francs. I'm sure that will do you good. We've done it and we've seen it grow and grow and grow.

Explore advertising sites and discover the many freelance opportunities available to you. You could earn extra income by doing paid assignments.

You can also set up your own shop and promote any product from home. I recommend the training and support provided by my friend Alphonse Affo, CEO of Exploits Motivations, who does excellent work in this area. He has enabled a number of young people in Africa to take charge of their lives, to avoid waiting for a physical employer and to be hired directly by company directors all over the world without having to travel. Today, from the comfort of your own home, you can work in a Canadian or even European company and be paid more adequately than if you were living in the West. You will have the opportunity to develop many qualities and skills. You can sacrifice a few free hours of the week to this wonderful freelancing activity.

You could open a fruit or bread stall at the weekend and earn a few resources a week, I mean it's not rocket science and you will be amazed at how easy it is.

I had fun listing the kinds of activities you can start with $17; it's just impressive!

Did you know that with $17, the equivalent of fifteen euros or twenty US dollars, you can own shares in several African, European and even American companies? I assure you that with fifteen euros, you can become a shareholder in any company on this planet earth. I invite you to look at financial market platforms such as **investing.com**; **https:// www.bvm-ac.org/horaires-seances-de- cotation/**; **https://www.brvm.org/fr/cours-actions/0**; or the platforms in North and South Africa.

Even if not everyone understands the stock market, it is still accessible and within everyone's reach. There are a few entities acting as a go-between between you and companies looking for funding to develop their activities. Wherever you are on planet earth, just type in your nearest stockbroker and you will find one to suit your needs. And I guarantee that after two or three years, if you are curious and want to put yourself at the service of your finances, you will end up operating on these markets independently. In any case, I can also guarantee you my services as a financial broker to help you build your financial future. If you want to operate in the sector, give yourself time to learn and understand the field. It's better to waste a few pennies learning about the field you want to invest in than to invest without any information at all.

I was talking to my brother, an agronomist, and I asked him how many kilograms of maize you need to sow on a hectare of land. He told me it was between 20 and 25 kilograms. I think that with $17 you can afford the 25kg to plant, perhaps on one of your parents' plots. It's true that $17 can't weed and maintain 1 hectare of maize crop, but that's to point out how much $17 can help you do, so don't scorn insignificant savings of $17 a month.

Pay off your first debt and so on.

In the next step, we will start paying off our first debt, which could be the $1,500 in funeral loans. Except for debt No. 1, you will only pay no more than the minimum amount due, on all other debts.

Some of you have been told that you need to pay a little more on each line of credit to get out of debt. However, it is essential to understand that this approach will not allow you to make any real progress. It didn't seem to make a dent in what we were doing. So again, pay the minimum monthly amount due on all other debts except debt No. 1. And then, because we have increased the amount to $180, instead of the planned amount to pay off debt No. 2, it may take eight months to set it up and so four months to clear it completely. That's true, because for debt No. 1, your minimum amount is $180. You take this extra $180that you have already got into the habit of paying on debt No. 1, and you apply it to debt No. 2. So instead of $180, you are going to pay $360; and instead of paying it off in eight months, it will take you four months to pay off debt No. 2.

But now you have got $360 more, because you have got the $180 you paid on debt No. 1 and the $180 you paid on this credit card debt on No. 2. Now you can tackle the next one.

Once again, we are starting with the shortest possible timeframe, because look! I've got rid of a debt, and that's one of the most important things that keeps your confidence up throughout the process. Congratulate yourself! Encourage yourself! Do something that gives you the joy of taking the next step. But celebrate.

Now that you have that visual quadrant in front of you, take a big red marker and put an X through it and when one of your debts is no longer on your record, it's done. Celebrate its disappearance.

Be creative and decide to create conditions to earn additional resources.

Except for your No. 1 debt, pay only the minimum monthly payment for each of your other debts.

For all your debts, make sure you only pay the minimum required each month, except for debt No. 1. Pay only the minimum monthly payment for all other debts and put the extra $170 or $350 on debt No. 1. So, for debt No. 1, you pay the minimum monthly payment plus the extra $17, $35, $90 or $180. Do this every month until debt No. 1 is paid off in full. Go to your graph and put a big red X on debt No. 1. You've done it!

K. Move on to the next debt as set out in your repayment plan.

Debt No. 2. Here's what you do:

Debt No. 1, you have paid $360 or $180 or even $17 per month. So, you go to debt No. 2. If you look in the notebook, debt No. 2 could be a repayment plan to your friend. You owe him $900, and your minimum monthly payment is $70.

Instead of paying only $70 each month, you will continue to pay what you were paying on debt No. 1. You will be paying one hundred and forty thousand a month on debt No. 2, and guess how long it will take to pay? Less than four months. It's done. You can celebrate. And you cross that one off.

Now you can move on to this debt No. 3, look in the binder and this may be the relative loan or the debt relating to your showroom equipment. Debt No. 3 is a minimum payment of $35. Add the $250 you were paying on debt No. 2; you're now paying $270 and your total debt then amounts to $1,700 – I'm taking my case for what I owed in 2019 -. It should have taken you ten months to pay off this debt but it will take you much less than that to pay it off if you continue to follow the process of adding to your new debt each time the amount you were paying from the smallest debt.

Obviously, it won't work if you pay off one debt and then go back into other debts, or pay off one or two and then go back to making the minimum payment or even the due date comes and, in your inability, or impossibility to pay, you take on a new debt to pay off the first one. You owe it to yourself to concentrate on eliminating each one of these debts or loans that you have until everything is wiped out, and if you follow this process, it should take you seven to eight years to completely wipe out even your home mortgage.

Most people tell me it takes five to eight years to get completely out of debt. For example, I read a story about a couple who had over $120,000 in debt, including their house. Their house was worth $75,000, so they had that amount of debt on top of it. By using this formula, $75,000 was paid off in full and it took them less than four and a half years to pay off their house completely. So, in about eight years, they were completely debt-free. The house payment alone would have taken them more than twenty years. With $170 a month and a lot of discipline to keep going, they succeeded.

You have managed to pay off debt No. 1, now move on to debt No. 2. For debt No. 2, pay the minimum monthly payment required for all the other debts, pay the minimum required for debt No. 2 plus the total amount you were paying on debt No. 1.

For example: for debt No. 2, your payments should be:

1. the monthly payment required for debt No. 2;

2. the minimum you paid on debt No. 1;

3. the extra $170 or $350.

You are now paying more than the minimum monthly payment and the extra $170 to $350. With each debt you pay off, you accelerate your payments on the next debt. Continue each month until your debt No. 2 is paid off. Go back to your debt table and put a big red X on debt No. 2. You've done it again.

Move on to debt No. 3.

For debt No. 3, you pay as follows:

1. the minimum monthly payment required for debt No. 3;

2. the total amount you previously paid on debt No. 2, which included:

    - the minimum monthly payment you previously paid on debt No. 2;
    - the minimum monthly payment you were paying on debt No. 1;
    - the additional $170 to $350 generated by your parallel activities.

Continue this process each month for each debt, always paying the minimum required plus everything you paid for previously repaid debts. Invest the final amount you have paid on your debt. Once you have paid off your last debt, take the total amount you paid on the last debt you paid off and invest it. Keep investing every month. This will be the start of your debt-free life and your financial success.

Remember that this is a process and for it to work, you have to stick with it month in month out. Don't quit the process because your chances of becoming debt-free will be very slim. Keep your spirits up and focus on a better future. If you feel like quitting, talk to a friend and your partner or financial adviser if you have one. Instead of arguing with your partner, seek advice from financial professionals. Remember, two minds are better than one.

'What do you do when you find yourself in a hole? Stop digging.'

Your seriousness will pay off.

Your seriousness will make your creditors trust you. If you respect your commitments, you will create a kind of trust between you and your creditors. Better still, you can have several credit cards that you use, but try to pay them off in full every month. I'm not one of those financial experts who will tell you to cut up your credit cards. You can have several cards that you use (and pay off in full) each month to accumulate points and thus ensure that you take advantage of the opportunities offered by the credit card companies. The trick is to make your monthly payments automatically, without having to worry about anything.

L. Reduce expenditure.

Some people have to cut back on their spending to get out of debt. As mentioned above, check your budget to see if there are any items that are less urgent than the peace of mind that paying off your debt will bring you. If not, look at each line item or, when an expense comes up, ask yourself if it will give you more peace of mind than paying off your existing debts. If so, pay it. If not, postpone it.

Chapter 8

CREATE WEALTH WITH THIS INGRAINED HABIT!

Once you have cleared your debts, don't stop. Now is the time to enjoy the discipline you have put in place to become financially free. Instead of going back to spending your money willy-nilly, continue to buy property, shares and bonds, but don't take out mutual life insurance, pension schemes or products to cover your children's future school fees.

I explained above what I would have earned on my plot of land in eight years if I decided to sell it today, compared with what I would have earned on the same savings in banks and insurance companies. There are two disadvantages to this: not only is the income low (4% at most), but you don't get to practise investing yourself. This will keep your financial IQ very low.

You will have money to invest even more, so your investment rate will rise from 10% to 30%, 50% and even 80% if you have to, and will be in the hundreds of thousands and tens of millions. So, you will have to keep reinvesting, and you will be living off the cash flow from your properties.

So, it's very interesting to see how this process starts to snowball. This will enable you to become rich more quickly. This process of deleveraging is the effective way in which you can become rich.

You may still have debts, but they will be good debts, and the rents and other income will pay them off for you. Thus, you will be able to tackle these debts with complete peace of mind. You will have lots of good debts, lots of debts linked to residential and commercial property, but these are good debts that will make you richer and richer.

If, for example, you paid $500 to pay off your last debt on your house, once that debt has been cleared, you still have that $500 every month. As I said, instead of going out and buying gadgets and all sorts of things (new fabrics, clothes, a new television set), you have $500 a month to invest. That's all you must do without really doing anything else.

Once again, that's the formula you can use. In this way, you will get out of bad debt, and that's what will help when you start investing to accumulate money.

In his book, *The Guide to Investing Money*, Robert Kiyosaki answers the question as to when we should start enjoying our money. His answer is this:

'Today, Kim and I have earned about seven of the cars, lots of houses, we travel on private jets and all that, but we have the cash flow from our investments that do that, not from our credit cards that pay for these things, and it's not the debt, it's the income that comes to us, constantly. So, our assets from our investments provide those spending lines and the reason why so many people have problems is because they buy the liability first, and then they try to buy assets, and that never happens because they keep buying other liabilities like cars, smartphones, houses for living and things like that.

By getting out of debt, bad debt, and then buying assets, your assets buy your liabilities, so you will always have a great lifestyle, and I mean an amazing lifestyle. The best part is you don't have to worry about money, you don't have to worry about anything, because you will always have more and more money no matter what because the process continues.' This process is well described in Robert Kiyosaki's book, which I highly recommend. In it, you will learn how to use small savings to acquire assets that, in turn, will generate substantial income to finance your liabilities.

Examine the possibility of finding other sources of income.

Many people have a job that simply doesn't pay enough to meet all their needs. Even if they spend wisely, they may need to find other sources of income to avoid going into debt.

One of the things that civil servants love is assignments. These are times when their employer offers them all expenses paid to go and do important work away from their place of work. Obviously, these are times when civil servants are away from their families and the daily routine. It's often time that could be put to good use doing other things that we wouldn't be able to do on site or in our place of residence. So, instead of turning these times into moments of holiday, revelry and fun, use them wisely to look for solutions to your financial situation.

In my case, stays abroad on mission are times of recollection and retreat. These are times that have always enabled me to make progress on one subject or another. In August 2019, I had the opportunity to go on a one-month mission trip to Yaoundé on a project aimed at facilitating mobility between African universities. This mobility mainly concerned students and, to a lesser extent, administrative staff. That's how I came to be selected to experience the University of Yaoundé's financial procedures. It was an opportunity for me to work on my calling, because for two years I was being taught about destiny, and one of the phrases that always motivated me was: 'Your fulfilment on earth is in your destiny'.

Did you know that? Very few people are fulfilled in their work or job and the vast majority work because they have to. We even go to training courses out of conformity, not out of an inner desire. In my search for my destiny, I took several in-person and audio courses, followed by tests and practical exercises. Completing these exercises enabled me to find my precise calling, and required prayer, concentration and calm.

I was definitely looking for some one-on-one time to work on the issue and I knew that my stay in Cameroon was going to be the perfect opportunity. When I arrived, I didn't have the opportunity to get to know the financial administration. On my first day, my hosts simply told me that mobility is an opportunity for agents to get a change of scenery and get to know universities, and that I had nothing to learn. I should rest, go for a walk and have a party. This free time allowed me to work on all my courses, tests and exercises. I read five books in a fortnight. I purchased the English versions of my favourite authors in a bookshop on the eve of my departure to say goodbye to my hosts. I found that it improved my English when I started to read the English versions of the books I'd read in French. In a fortnight, I achieved what I couldn't achieve back in Benin for twelve months. This book that is currently in your hands is one such achievement.

I realised that I would be more fulfilled by helping people to solve their money problems, not necessarily by setting up a business. If you need to develop a specific talent within yourself, go ahead, find the school that can offer it and train yourself. There are things inside you that you're passionate about. Look for them, work on them and suggest them to those around you. I like figures, I like interpreting and analysing situations and I like earning money. I realise that I would be fulfilled and rich if I helped a lot of people to solve their problems with numbers and, above all, with money. The aim is to find practical solutions to the difficult financial situations people face.

The first thing I realised was that I needed training in financial analysis and financial engineering. There was no school in my country where I could get that kind of expertise. A year later, I landed on distance learning in financial engineering and this training cost me two years of Internet packages and more than three million in training fees. - You can't afford such training without first putting something aside for such occasions, hence the need to keep something in your income.

My ultimate dream is to see a world where people solve their money problems easily. Many things come to mind, but now it's debt that I was inspired to tackle first. And I can see that it's well-founded, because a lot of people who claim to be financial freedom coaches rush in on concepts such as financial gain without dwelling on what's really preventing people from freeing themselves and unleashing their own potential: debt.

My plan is to encourage people to get out of debt and become financially comfortable. Being wealthy doesn't just mean having lots of money, it means being able to support yourself without going into debt. If you find yourself in a situation of poverty, you may need to go into debt to cover your basic needs, or you may not be making the right financial choices. For example, this could mean refusing to provide yourself with quality care in the event of illness. My aim is to help you adopt a more responsible approach to your finances so that you can live a more fulfilling life.

Put your ingenuity to work for your personal finances.

Your ingenuity can be your ability to play football or gamble, to woo, to sing, to perform, all things that you find easy to do.

See how difficult it is for many to woo a woman. And yet it's easy or exciting for others. By doing so, not only are you wasting your three most important resources (time, money and vigour) but it doesn't earn you anything. However, others who find this difficult need it to start a family. You can offer your solutions in the art of approaching your partner or work on the possibility of becoming a couples coach or writing a book in the field.

Interpreting or debriefing football matches: I have a brother living in Benin, but he knows all the possible tactical plans that the Barcelona or Real Madrid team can put in place to beat a rival. He hardly misses a game. I suppose it's a passion for him. Why not take a parallel course to become a football coach or players' agent and make this refined talent available to a professional club?

Do you have a knack for dancing or a lot of other things? Take a popular song, suggest a dance step and publish it on social networks. YouTube will pay you if the video is serious and is followed by more than five thousand people. People will request your page for advertising. That's money for you. Do you like reading? Make a summary of your reading and publish it, or turn it into a video and post it on your social networks.

Do you enjoy spending time with God's Word? Share the fruit of your meditations. It will save someone from some kind of trouble. Even if you gain nothing, you will certainly bring something to someone. It's not free in God's eyes.

Are you a cartoonist? Draw portraits of the authorities in your country. Look out for events to which they are invited and come and exhibit. They will be flabbergasted and contact you for a formal contract. In short, put your ingenuity to good use.

Put your passions to work for your finances.

Whether men or women, we all have something we are passionate about that uses up our time. Take a close look at your daily life and see what takes up your time outside of your family and work. For most men, it's football, for women it's soap operas, and for both, it's music and social networking. Ask yourself how you can use your passion to generate money. Your passion is a source of blessing for someone. Try to make money from your passions.

Take moments of debt as opportunities to increase your financial intelligence.

When you find yourself in debt, think of it as an opportunity to solve a financial problem. Just as you get stronger by solving mathematical exercises, so you get better and better at solving your money problems. The same applies to physical exercise and sport. At first, it's hard to do one or two juggling moves, or two to ten push-ups, or ten to twenty sit-ups. But the more you repeat these exercises, the easier they become, and the better you feel.

Financial problems are no different. Just as other exercises allow us to move from one year to the next (maths, for example) or to succeed in a field (top-level sport) or to keep our bodies away from health problems, so facing our money problems takes us from one stage to the next if we accept or decide to face them.

Chapter 9

BREAK THE HEREDITARY CIRCLE OF PRECARIOUSNESS AND RESTORE THE FINANCIAL FLOW OF JUSTICE.

The circle of insecurity and the financial flow of injustice are the yokes that prevent abundance from flowing into our lives. Break them!

Avoid behaviour in the circle of insecurity.

The circle of insecurity is a system of thought that needs to be eradicated from our minds and from our daily behaviour if we are to adopt a new attitude to managing our finances.

The mentality behind this behaviour is that fathers and mothers are content to look after their first children in the hope that when they are settled somewhere, they will be able to look after them - parents - and their younger brothers and sisters. I will explain this attitude in four phases.

The cycle or circle consists of 4 phases, repeated from one generation to another. Here's what it looks like:

Phase 1: Your current attitude

I'm not particularly familiar with your story, but all stories come together in one way or another. You remember how you got to where you are today. You are undoubtedly the product of a great deal of sacrifice, self-sacrifice and courage on the part of both your parents and yourself. Your parents may have had to sacrifice their comfort or even their necessities to push you to a certain level. Some people just couldn't manage it, and the child you were was forced to work to support your schooling or training. Worse still, others have grown up without one or even both parents, leading a very complicated life.

Everyone has a story. Mine is special. For others, it's even more so. I spent ten years with my maternal uncle, far from my parents. It wasn't easy, but I bless the Lord for the wonderful father he was to me and the wonderful family I grew up in. In this environment, I developed a lot of skills that I wouldn't have had if I'd grown up with my parents. These skills helped me a lot in adult life when I had to face working life.

When you have gone through childhood situations such as those described above and you end up changing your status, you become a source of joy and pride for yourself, your family and the world around you. Just because, by God's grace, we have managed to land a good job or set up a business that's beginning to bear fruit, we often rush into consumer spending in order to satisfy our desires, to keep up with the Joneses.

This is how we start acquiring the things we need to survive, such as a car, designer clothes, expensive outings to restaurants, bars, nightclubs etc., consumer goods, high rent with all its amenities, help for relatives, friends and so on. And here, as a young employee or entrepreneur, your income can more or less cover these expenses. And if you are one of the eldest members of your family, you should start preparing to take care of your younger brothers at school, because at the moment your parents may already be close to retirement and gradually finding it difficult to bear the costs of your younger brothers' secondary school or university education.

Phase 2: Changing your marital status increases your standard of living

That's right! Is your heart starting to beat for someone? Congratulations and welcome to married life. Your change of status means a change in a lot of things in your life. First of all, if you're serious about doing things the normal way, it's important for you to complete the formalities with your in-laws before you get your hands on the young lady. This includes everything from the dowry to the wedding ceremony. For the most modest weddings, you can spend at least $1,700, including the dowry.

On top of all this, there are the expenses for conveniences and other things, such as a car, furniture, designer clothes and shoes, other excessive wedding expenses, expensive outings, consumer goods, rent (moving house), help for the two sets of parents, and unhealthy competition - between brothers and sisters or between husbands of sisters of the same blood.

Phase 3: Children's expenses increase the bill over the years

I have heard that the arrival of a child in a couple increases the couple's spending budget by at least 20%. If you don't want to change your financial habits, make sure you increase your spending budget by at least 20% every time before you welcome a new baby into the family.

Welcoming a baby in the couple also means additional expenses. From pregnancy to childbirth and everything that goes with it, it's a considerable sum to be prepared to spend. Then there are the expenses associated with celebrating the birth of the heir or heiress in the family cercle, the baby shower and later on, the daily milk, and so on. As years go by, the expenses associated with organising birthdays, schooling, various celebrations and holidays are added to the income, which is becoming increasingly insufficient. This creates excessive debt, and the ageing of the parents (care, support and medical expenses) adds to the conflicts within the couple. This is the case, for example, when you manage to pay for your father's medical expenses but find yourself unable to pay for your mother-in-law's consultation fees. All this leads to you going deeper and deeper into debt, not to mention the costs of burying one of your parents.

Phase 4: All this prevents you from saving properly for your children's future

When you manage to meet all these pressing needs daily, you worry less and less about putting something aside for your retirement and to finance your children's education. As a result, you start saving late, pay off recurring debts and are unable to finance your children's education. Some people manage to finance their first children's education properly, in the hope that when they are settled they will take care of their younger brothers. And if the first children don't manage to settle down quickly - and even if they do, their own needs prevent them from doing so - the other children are forced to make do with training courses that are unsuited to their profiles. Children inherit difficult living and studying conditions. You manage to get by and the cycle starts all over again for these children.

You are the fruit of this cycle and your current behaviour tends to reproduce exactly the same thing, generation after generation. This cycle of insecurity prevents children from developing and fulfilling their potential. If you don't take yourself seriously, if you don't start putting money aside and if you don't start developing new sources of income, your children will suffer the cycle of insecurity.

Just think! Your parents are still alive and you know that, in the normal order of things, you'll be in charge of burying them. How much are you putting aside for this big day of big expenses? Where are you going to find the money if not by borrowing? Are you going to borrow money again from your current situation, mortgaging your children's future? I think your children deserve better, because even bad people want good things for their children.

*'Or which of you, if his son asks for bread, will give him a stone? Or if he asks for fish, will he give him a serpent? (**Matthew 7:9-10**)*

*'Or if he asks for an egg, will he give him a scorpion?' (**Luke11:12**)*

By refusing to finance your children's education properly, what are you giving them? Stone or bread? An egg or a scorpion? I don't think your children deserve to be treated in this way, because the wicked don't inflict such things on their children (***Luke 11:13***), and you can't afford to do so. I believe that you are a good parent who also seeks the good of his or her children.

*'A good man leaves an inheritance to his children's children. (**Proverbs 13:22**)*

*'But if anyone does not provide for his relatives, and especially for members of his household, he has denied the faith and is worse than an unbeliever.' (**1 Timothy 5:8**)*

You become wise when you behave in this way. You work tirelessly with a view to leaving a legacy not for your children, but for your grandchildren. If you do this, at least you are freeing your children from many pressures and giving them the opportunity to stretch and fulfil themselves. In this way, you are fulfilling God's will!

Your children are blessings in your quiver. You must do all you can to equip yourself with what you need to push them as far as possible, because they are like arrows in the hands of the warrior that you are.

*'Like arrows in the hands of a warrior are the children of one's youth.' (**Psalms 127:4**)*

Break the cycle of precariousness by starting to completely reorganise your finances. The success of your posterity depends on it!

Over and above these things, there is a direct correlation between overspending, having too much debt and having a low savings rate. In the context of savings, debt has a cost. The money that repays the debt and goes to creditors is money that cannot be used for anything else. This is what we call the 'opportunity cost' of debt. Compare borrowing $170,000 and paying 12% interest (i.e. $200) with saving $170,000 and investing them at 6% ($100). The real economic benefit is 18% ($300).

Restore the financial flow of justice.

Debt is a form of slavery.

When you owe your creditor money that you have not returned, in one way or another, you are effectively their slave. Debt is slavery, it's a curse. It's oppression. Several debtors have been summoned to court. Even in the Koran, a debtor can be imprisoned. Moreover, the person who is in debt is not free. He is free to move around, but not free in his heart. In the Bible, people in debt are sentenced to imprisonment if they don't get their debt forgiven. The story of a prophet's wife in the Bible is edifying:

'Now the wife of one of the sons of the prophets cried to Elisha, "Your servant my husband is dead, and you know that your servant feared the Lord; but the creditor has come to take my two children to be his slaves.' (**2 Kings 4:1**)

Similarly, one of Jesus' parables also relates to the imprisonment of debtors. You will find a collection of Bible verses relating to debt at the end of this book.

Debt is crippling.

The Bible is not silent about debt. Obviously, there were no bank cards or automatic loans in Jesus' day, but lending and borrowing were part of the economic landscape of His day. The Bible does not strictly prohibit debt, but it does consider it a form of slavery (**Proverbs 22:7**).

'The wicked borrows but does not pay back; but the righteous is generous and gives.' (**Psalms 37:21**)

There is a glass ceiling, an invisible ceiling that prevents you from taking possession of your finances.

'...and the borrower is the slave of the lender'. (**Proverbs 22:7**)

There is a bond of slavery between the lender and the borrower. It is a form of slavery that is invisible but real and tangible.

The verse above only applies to you when you borrow money and don't pay it back. You are a slave to the person who lent you the money. But there is never a slave whose condition is superior to that of his or her master. At best, a slave is equal to his or her master.

When you borrow money from someone who has trusted you, you put a master/slave system on your life. Every time the person who lent you money has a need that can't be met because of your failure to repay, the vice tightens on your life and your finances because the slave is no better off than his or her master. Many people languish in financial difficulties and/or suffer because of this bond of slavery. If you see your creditor's life, don't think that yours is better than his or hers. If you see your creditor's life and you don't like it, be quick to pay them back. Otherwise, your situation will never improve because there is a cry, a pattern of injustice that rises up to God. Your financial ceiling is limited when you don't pay, even if your creditor doesn't chase you up because of his or her modesty. The fact remains that the contents of this verse apply. If the person doesn't succeed in their finances and their projects, it's because you won't succeed either. What I'm talking about has been tried and tested, and many have applied it and found favour with God. If the person doesn't succeed financially, you won't succeed either, because a slave's situation is linked to that of his or her master.

When you put a plan in place that you begin to respect, you cancel out the condemnations in this verse. So, I invite you to grab a blank sheet of paper and write down the names of everyone you owe and the amount owed. Even if it hurts, do it.

Call each of these people to ask for their forgiveness. Tell them earnestly: I ask for your forgiveness because at some point in my life I had difficulties and you reached out to me, but I failed to honour my commitment. Instead, I ran away, I stuck my head in the sand and that spoiled the relationship we had.' Ask them to forgive you for not having lived up to the trust they placed in you and pledge to pay them back. That's how you will undo the invisible straitjacket of money that's blocking your life. The stranglehold will be lifted. Make a commitment to repay little by little on a regular basis.

In my country, Benin, it's generally said that when you move into your new house, you have serious problems meeting your most basic needs. I have witnessed this in the lives of many relatives and colleagues who, after moving into their new homes, went without food for months on end. They have experienced inexplicable situations: illnesses, inability to meet minimum expenses, household and children's costs, and so on.

When I saw people close to me going through this, I promised myself and asked God that it would never happen to me. To that end, I tried to make a number of investments that could start to generate income before committing to building my main residence. Personally, I never believed in this reality until the day I experienced it first-hand when I built my house. I can assure you that I, who never had to worry about food or meeting my small expenses for more than 8 years in a row when I had a stable professional status, experienced several days when I started the day without a penny. I would end the day without bringing any food home.

We lived through some extraordinary situations in our past, before I started working. Before I took up a permanent job, we would even lack 1 dime to buy coal to make a fire. There were times when my wife went out around the house where we had rented looking for pieces of coal to make fire and cook a handful of leftover beans, if only to put something in the belly before another day of hope arrived.

We routinely ate maize dough with no sauce on top of it but chilli and mustard as we didn't have the money to afford fish. I'd like to appreciate my wife for this moment that we went through without our fellow tenants even noticing. We got through it without any discontent, without any insults, without any falling out. I can assure you that this situation returned between September 2020 and 29 April 2021, as I was writing these lines. It's true that we didn't go looking for lumps of coal this time around, but there were several days when we didn't find anything to eat all day. As the person who used to pay for the children's schooling before the start of the new school year, I was threatened that my children would be expelled from school if the school accounts didn't balance out to zero. Several times I was forced to fast because I had nothing in my pocket to eat at break time. It was when I was researching the slave-like relationship between debtors and creditors that I realised that I myself was still indebted to a lot of people in this kind of situation.

In fact, I owed the head builder, who in turn owed his apprentices and other people who had been called in to work on the construction site of my property. I still owed $235 to the plasterer, and even small sums to other tradesmen. I owed $500 to my mother-in-law, which I borrowed for the funeral ceremonies of a relative during the same period. Even though this lady's situation was not exactly glowing, she didn't have the courage to claim her debt from me, given all the things I had done for her; but she needed her money back and was in deep trouble. You can understand that in this case, where I owed my mother-in-law three hundred thousand, my situation could not have been better than hers, especially as the money I borrowed from her was the proceeds of a plot of land sold for her abroad, and for which she fought body and soul to get this part of the sale.

It was then that I came to see that it was because I owed people who were struggling to make ends meet on a daily basis that my financial situation was similar to theirs. It's true that you couldn't see it, but deep down I had all the problems that people like that, who lived solely from their daily work, had. I owed a lot. I didn't know how to get out of it. I was tired and all I did was sleep when I got home. Things were kind of stuck. I couldn't even find a way out.

I had even been in debt for a year to someone to whom I'd entrusted some of the research for this book. I didn't pay the man back after several reminders, so I didn't make any progress on the book. I was inexplicably stuck. I wasn't doing much, but

I wasn't making any progress on the book either. I have to remind you that this gentleman lost his job in the meantime and a few days later his mother. Can you imagine his difficulties? On a daily basis, he lived off the little tasks he found. Even when I tried to pay for them, I couldn't find the money. And the expenses were piling up, but my situation was getting worse by the day because the commitments and expenses were there.

I came to realise that my situation was critical because I was still in slavery with these people and, as a slave can never be in a better situation than his master, my situation had not changed and all I did was get stressed out and angry every time I saw the phone calls, WhatsApp messages and signs from my creditors.

When I discovered this secret, I decided to break through this ceiling and re-establish the financial flow of justice. I started by paying back the $500 to my mother-in-law. I called the bricklayer at home and humbly tried to explain to him why I hadn't paid him in the seven months since I'd moved into the house he'd built for me. I owed him $1,500. I gave him $500 and promised to pay the rest over the next two months, $500 on the 25th of May and June. I drew up a repayment plan for all the other creditors and I can assure you that a lot of odd things started to disappear from my life. I started waking up very early to work on my book and began to find ways of moving forward with my projects.

If you are in debt to certain people who have the same financial situation or a lower lifestyle than you, pay them off as quickly as possible; otherwise, you will obviously think that you are better off than them, but in truth, you are no better off spiritually or financially than they are. And for goodness' sake, don't owe those who directly or indirectly carry the load of the daily routine with you. Pay systematically and without the least reserve your servants, handymen and drivers and more generally your employees who often do the heavy lifting. If you can't call, have the courage to go and see these people. Make a commitment and stick to it. That way you will cancel out the blockage in your life.

If you do, you'll see the financial miracle that will happen in your life. I'm talking about a sincere act of forgiveness and commitment. The efforts you've been making that weren't working will start to bear fruit. Do it and leave me your testimony at www.ayanouhubert.com or on my Facebook handle.

I pray that the Lord grant you the grace to start implementing the financial flow of justice and that where heavy obstacles, blockage was weighing on your life, that the application remove the condemnation and that you regain your financial clarity. May anyone living in this situation have the grace to put an end to this bond of slavery so that the weight on their finances be broken. Lord, may Your grace come upon their lives and may the weight on their lives be lifted. Grant them the grace to believe in the application of Your Word and may this financial burden be lifted forever.

Make this prayer with me

Lord, Eternal Father, Father of love, of compassion, of goodness, we want to thank You because Your Word brings us deliverance and light, for it is the truth. Father of grace, I pray for my beloved brothers and sisters who are reading this book and praying this prayer with me.

I pray, Lord, that You grant them the grace to begin setting up the financial stream of justice to contact these people, ask their sincere forgiveness and commit to repaying the funds they have borrowed.

Lord, I pray that Your hand of grace and favour be extended to each and every one of them, and that where blockages were persistent, where a burden was weighing on their lives, blocking or capping their finances and reducing them to nothing, that because of their obedience, this weight be lifted and their finances may flourish again or simply blossom.

Lord, grant them the grace not to be seduced by false reasoning, by seductive thoughts that would prevent them from taking any other path but the path of obedience to Your Word. May each of us be led to obey Your Word and to enjoy its fruit.

Thank You, Lord, that You are granting them multiple graces and that the application of Your Word is removing the obvious obstacles. May their finances be restored, and may they be able to raise their heads financially. May the years that were devoured by the locust be granted to them again by Your hands and Your goodness.

Thank You Father for doing this, in Jesus' name. Amen.

Chapter 10

TO GET

EVEN

FASTER...

Giving your tithe helps you.

If you want to quickly restore the financial flow of justice and regain the lustre of your finances, join with the privileged partner, the owner of gold, silver and all creation. Trust God by giving your tithes and making offerings. Rest assured. I haven't started a church and I don't have that heartbeat, at least that's not where I plan to make my fortune. And this book is not intended to be theoretical or to hold back certain truths that have been tested and approved by many rich people.

Let me give you an exercise.

Starting today, identify the rich man who impresses you, whom you like to be like. Select three to five people and try to find out, through their stories, how they built their fortune. If you can't trace how these people made their fortune, I ask you to remove them from your list and add new people. If at the end of your search you find that the people you want to be like have not trusted God, if they have not entered into a partnership or have God as their partner, then you may not consider the advice given in this last chapter. But if these people have had the Lord Jesus as their partner, then I advise you and recommend that you do not depart from it.

Let me help you before you go and do your own research. I have had the difficult task of examining the history and lives of the people I want to be like. Many rich, successful, fulfilled and happy people have trusted God to build their fortunes.

Put God to the test.

One of the passages in the Bible that upset me when I started reading it was *Malachi 3:10-12*. It says that the Lord God said:

'10 Bring the full tithe into the storehouse, that there may be food in my house; and thereby put me to the test, says the Lord of hosts, if I will not open the windows of heaven for you and pour down for you a blessing until there is no more need. 11 I

will rebuke the devourer for you, so that it will not destroy the fruit of your soil, and your vine in the field shall not fail to bear, says the Lord of hosts. 12 Then all nations will call you blessed, for you will be a land of delight, says the Lord of hosts.'

I went through the Bible from Genesis to Revelation. This is the only time the Lord says to test him. God says to test him. Why not give it a try?

I advise you to try. The Bible goes further and says:

'God is not a man, that he should lie, a son of man, that he should change his mind. Has he said, and will he not do it? Or has he spoken and will he not fulfil it? **(Numbers 23:19)**

I made these two verses my horse for getting out of debt. It was after that that I discovered everything I presented to you in this book. I advise you to give it a try. And if in the end it doesn't work, you will have tried it. But it really does work, it always works, because what God has said, He does, because He is not a liar. Amen!

Your tithes and offerings are not an expense, they are an investment, a seed (**Matthew 6:19-21**).

An expense is a definitive consumption. An investment is an investment for future income. **Malachi 3:10-12** speaks of the multiplication of pennies given. So, your tithe is not a permanent deduction from your income, but an investment for a multiplied harvest or a plantation from which fruit will be harvested that you can use to pay off your debts and build your financial empire.

Tithing is to income or wages what a seed is to an orange or a pit to a mango. I don't know anyone who eats a mango with its stone or swallows the seeds of an orange. The tithe is that part of your salary that you must not consume. It's the pit or the seed of your wages. If you eat it, you block the cycle of abundant reproduction in your life. Just as a seed can provide acres of orange trees, so tithing gives you the ability to multiply your finances.

The five blessings of tithing

When you tithe, you place yourself under a divine covenant that gives you the following five blessings according to *Malachi 3:10-12*.

When you tithe, this is what happens:

1. The Lord opens the floodgates of heaven upon you, that is to say, you operate under open skies. Heaven is no longer closed to your prayers;
2. The Lord showers blessings on you in abundance;
3. The Lord threatens those who devour your finances and they will no longer destroy the fruits of the earth;
4. Your vineyard will never be barren; in other words, everything you do will bear fruit;
5. All nations will call you blessed, for you will be a land of delight.

Six biblical principles for saving and investing your money

Many Christians know that they need to save and invest for their retirement. But many find it difficult to adopt a practical methodology for managing their money, especially when it comes to saving and investing for a distant and uncertain future.

This is a difficult question because it opens up many perspectives. Some advocate a life of deprivation, avoiding all luxuries and savings because of the Kingdom. Others suggest setting up a budget, avoiding debt, and advocating regular savings with the aim of being better off and being able to give and spend later in life. I would like to invite you to focus on extreme frugality and saving so that you can retire before the age of 40.

Here are seven biblical principles that might help you with the question of how to arrive at a personal theology about money that balances biblical orthodoxy with setting aside savings and investments for the future.

1) Setting aside for future needs is biblical.

Some Christians don't put money aside for retirement because they believe it's disobedience (they usually quote *Matthew 6:19-20*), or because they feel guilty putting money aside when others are in need. Others believe they don't need to, because God will take care of them (*Isaiah 46:4*). Still others would like to save, but spend everything they have set aside (*Proverbs 13:18*).

You may be surprised to learn that saving is actually encouraged in the Bible. Scripture endorses saving for known, anticipated future needs (*Genesis 41*; *Proverbs 6:6-11*; *Proverbs 21:5*; *Proverbs 21:20*).

The Bible teaches that it is possible to save and invest wisely for the future while also being 'rich for God' by 'storing up treasures in heaven' (*Luke 12: 21*; *Matthew 6:19-21*).

2) Saving honours God and serves others.

It would be easy to see saving as a purely selfish activity. That may be the case - we only have to read the text about the rich fool in *Luke 12* - but it shouldn't be.

Saving honours God by treating money as a gift that has been given to us (*James 1:16-17*). Instead of indulging in unplanned, impulsive or foolish spending, wise saving demonstrates the importance we attach to managing our gifts well (*Luke 12:47-48*).

Proper stewardship will put you in a better position to help when great needs arise (*Ephesians 4:28*). You'll be able to respond more quickly and, perhaps, more meaningfully (*Proverbs 3:27*). Saving may also allow you to leave a legacy, as a blessing to your heirs, so that they can be a blessing to others (*Proverbs 13:22*).

3) Procrastination is a mistake.

We all have a tendency to put things off until tomorrow. But if you don't save soon enough, you'll miss out on one of the most powerful financial forces: tax-free compound interest, or interest earnings.

On 10 February 2021 I attended a financial workshop at my church where the facilitator, Pastor Teddy, seriously motivated us to start saving, to put something aside, no matter how small. He even prayed for us. He asked us to start saving right away (the workshop is available on the YouTube page of the *Impact Centre Chrétien* church in Cotonou). We were motivated and I'm sure many of us had made resolutions. I'd like to know where each of the participants stands today.

Personally, I left the meeting with the commitment to deposit a standing order for a transfer from my account to an investment account on the following Monday, a resolution that was firmly taken. But let me tell you that it was four months later that I actually deposited the transfer. And yet I was convinced, determined and motivated by the idea of making deductions from my income for a savings account. So, there's no point in being motivated and determined; you have to really start. If you don't start, you won't succeed, no matter how committed you are at the outset.

Most people put off saving because they think that waiting is unimportant. On the contrary, they wait until they have more disposable income later, or they have more pressing immediate needs - including paying debts, low wages, health care expenses or the need to put money aside for a child's education. They plan to start saving later.

But even if things change later, the money set aside later for retirement will at least have time to multiply (*Matthew 25:27*). Start by doing only what you can and increase over time.

Did you know that saving ten thousand a month will give you at least six hundred thousand after five years? What does ten thousand represent in your monthly income? And yet you can't hold it back to have six hundred thousand in capital at the end of five years to start a business.

4) A wise investment is right and good.

Investing is not just about stock market transactions. It's not betting on a good plan that your brother-in-law told you about. Such speculation is like betting on future events, and more often than not you will lose more than you gain (*Proverbs 28:19*; *1 Timothy 6:10*).

Investing is indeed necessary if it is done wisely. It means putting money into real businesses that employ people and provide products and services to consumers. Fortunately, the companies we invest in do their job well and provide us with a return commensurate with our investment (*Proverbs 31:10-31*; *Ecclesiastes 11:1-6*). Don't let yourself be led into risky investments. Look for promising sectors.

Most of us would do well to invest in low-cost, passively managed, mutual and exchange-traded index funds rather than individually managing stocks and bonds. We also need to keep an eye on the big fees and expenses they generate, which can have serious consequences if they are not sufficiently diversified (assets that balance each other out) or by buying and selling at the wrong time (because of your emotions) or by lacking knowledge about our investments (don't buy what you don't understand or invest in an area that is foreign to you).

5) Saving can be a source of temptation.

We can be tempted to save for the wrong reasons - out of fear, greed, or a desire not to depend on God and others. If you save because of fear, then you are not trusting God (*1 Timothy 6:17*). If you do it out of greed, you have missed the point entirely (*Proverbs 1:19*; *Mark 8:36*; *Luke 12:15*). And once you have acquired some wealth, you don't want to become like the miser *Ecclesiastes 5:13* tells us about or the 'rich fool' *Luke 12* tells us about. The problem with these two characters is not that they saved, but that they thought only of themselves and put their faith in wealth rather than in God.

Hoarders are consumed by the need to preserve their wealth rather than risk it for productive uses and the good of others. This also brings curses (***Proverbs 11:26***) and judgement (***Luke 12:16-21***; ***James 5:3***; ***Psalms 39:6***; ***Ecclesiastes 5: 13***; ***Zechariah 9:3***).

6) Balance is the key

Finding the right balance is the key. On the one hand, we need to set something aside and invest it wisely for our future needs. On the other, we want to be generous and remain dependent on God, recognising that He is the source of our provision and that He alone controls the future. Whatever our decisions, they should come from a heart full of gratitude to God for His kind generosity to us - a God who is gracious, loving and merciful (***Psalms 107:8-9***) - and based on the biblical wisdom He has given us on the subject. Could He have multiplied them?

The seven biblical conditions for using credit

a) Be determined to repay the loan. (***Romans 13:7***)

When you borrow money, be determined to pay it back. Don't let thoughts of trying not to repay your loan get into your mind.

b) Never cosign. (***Proverbs 17:18***)

Yes, don't cosign a debt. The person for whom you vouch may not be willing or may find it difficult to pay. In this case, you will be sued for repayment of a sum that you did not have before. This can have a negative impact on your finances and those of your family.

c) Keep your commitments. (*Proverbs 22:26-27*)

Make achievable or tenable commitments and stick to them. This builds confidence in you and in your partners.

d) Avoid making commitments based on future income. (*Proverbs 27:1*)

Make commitments based on reliable income. It's true that there is no such thing as 100% certainty, but make commitments based on certainty and reasonableness. Do not make commitments based on a promise or on the winnings of a game of chance.

e) Never put your family at risk. (*1Thimothy 5:8*)

The Bible says that anyone who does not take care of his family has denied the faith; he is worse than an unbeliever. I say that anyone who makes financial decisions without regard for his family is worse than an unbeliever. When making important financial decisions, consider the consequences for your family.

f) Avoid consumer debt. (*Romans 13:8*)

This book is mainly about this. Most bad debts are consumer debts. Avoid them.

g) Use credit wisely. (*1 Corinthians 4:2*)

The credit you take is an opportunity to achieve an important situation that will enable you to progress in your activity to the happiness of those around you. Manage it like a good father.

Finally, I'd like to share a thought I read on Mr Aimé Egla's LinkedIn page. I find it very interesting and it may also help you:

'Bank loan... let's talk about it!

A civil servant approaches his bank to apply for a loan of $25,000. Here are the figures for the loan:

- $25,000 repayable over 7 years (84 months).

- $1,600 in insurance costs,

- $375 administration fees,

- $50 pledge account,

- $400 (monthly instalments) x 84.

Total repayment: $36,000.

That is $11,000 in interest repaid...

Bank Loans: Solution Or Suffocation?

Bank Loans: Intelligent Debt?

No one is forcing us to do this, only necessity leads us to it.

Bank loans are OPTIONAL for employees. The bank pays us our salary, in return for interest, and offers us SAVINGS and/or a LOAN.

However, it has to be said that the loan is expensive, too expensive, and so expensive that it becomes a burden.

The employee whose transferable portion (1/3 of salary) is retained for 7 years and who finally repays not far from 40% of the capital borrowed, for 13 million received, will pay 21.

If ever there's a hard blow, the door is open to the 'lizards' because, when you owe your bank, you lose all your rights. All you have left is the option of redemption, and then it's a case of Scylla and Charybdis!

I hear you say 'if the money borrowed is put to good use'... Yes, but it's the COST of the loan that really needs to be reviewed, with its asphyxiating fees and interest rates!

I can 'use a loan well', without having invested it in a business with an immediate return. For example, setting up a plantation, paying for my children's education, buying land, starting a building site...

Bank loans are ultimately DANGEROUS for employees who have no other resources, and beware of those who squander their loan on a building without being able to finish it... He'll be 'telling time' in the rubble of his building site....

I owe it to my younger brothers to tell them the truth, and I hate double-talk.

Never get into debt to please yourself, save for that!

Don't get into debt for more than 24 months - it's a terrible trap!

Don't get into debt for an investment where the return won't immediately make up for the painful repayments.

Don't listen to the advice of 'financial theorists' and the like - real life is different.

Prefer saving, by all means, including your tontines, and avoid bank loans of more than 2 years.

Experts know what I'm talking about, and success stories are just exceptions.

But, as everyone knows their own reality and as long as Maaadou is not Digbeu, what works for one can be catastrophic for another!

You've been warned: SAVE rather than BORROWING. Life is beautiful, let's cherish it.

Collection of Bible verses about debt and wealth

*'Now the wife of one of the sons of the prophets cried to Elisha, "Your servant my husband is dead, and you know that your servant feared the LORD, but the creditor has come to take my two children to be his slaves.' (**2 Kings 4:1**)*

'Be not one of those who give pledges, who put up security for debts.' (**Proverbs 22:26**)

'Shall not all these take up their taunt against him, with scoffing and riddles for him, and say, "Woe to him who heaps up what is not his own-- for how long?-- and loads himself with pledges!' (**Habakkuk 2:6**)

'The rich rules over the poor, and the borrower is the slave of the lender.' (**Proverbs 22:7**)

'The wicked borrows but does not pay back, but the righteous is generous and gives;' (**Psalms 37:21**)

'If you lie down, you will not be afraid; when you lie down, your sleep will be sweet.' (**Proverbs 3:24**)

'When he began to settle, one was brought to him who owed him ten thousand talents. 25 And since he could not pay, his master ordered him to be sold, with his wife and children and all that he had, and payment to be made. 26 So the servant fell on his knees, imploring him, 'Have patience with me, and I will pay you everything.' 27 And out of pity for him, the master of that servant released him and forgave him the debt.' (**Matthew 18:24-27**)

'Bring the full tithe into the storehouse, that there may be food in my house. And thereby put me to the test, says the LORD of hosts, if I will not open the windows of heaven for you and pour down for you a blessing until there is no more need. 11 I will rebuke the devourer for you, so that it will not destroy the fruits of your soil, and your vine in the field shall not fail to bear, says the LORD of hosts. 12 Then all nations will call you blessed, for you will be a land of delight, says the LORD of hosts.' (**Malachi 3: 10-12**)

'19 Do not lay up for yourselves treasures on earth, where moth and rust destroy and where thieves break in and steal, 20 but lay up for yourselves treasures in heaven, where neither moth nor rust destroys and where thieves do not break in *and steal. 21 For where your treasure is, there your heart will be also.' (**Matthew 6:19-21**)*